BAKING

BAKING

Over **140** delicious recipes, **500** color photographs,
STEP-BY-STEP images, and **NUTRITIONAL INFORMATION**

First published in 2012
LOVE FOOD is an imprint of Parragon Books Ltd

Parragon
Queen Street House
4 Queen Street
Bath BA1 1HE, UK

www.parragon.com/lovefood

ISBN: 978-1-4454-6572-2

Printed in China

Cover and additional design by Geoff Borin
New photography by Clive Streeter
New food styling by Angela Drake and Sally Streeter
Introduction, new recipes, and notes by Angela Drake
Nutritional analysis by Fiona Hunter

Notes for the Reader
This book uses standard kitchen measuring spoons and cups. All spoon and cup
measurements are level unless otherwise indicated. Unless otherwise stated,
milk is assumed to be whole, eggs are large, individual vegetables are medium,
and pepper is freshly ground black pepper. Unless otherwise stated, all root
vegetables should be washed and peeled before using.

Garnishes and serving suggestions are all optional and not necessarily included
in the recipe ingredients or method. The times given are only an approximate
guide. Preparation times differ according to the techniques used by different
people and the cooking times may also vary from those given. Optional
ingredients, variations, or serving suggestions have not been included in
the time calculations.

Recipes using raw or very lightly cooked eggs should be avoided by infants, the
elderly, pregnant women, and people with weakened immune systems. Pregnant
and breast-feeding women are advised to avoid eating peanuts and peanut
products. People with nut allergies should be aware that some of the prepared
ingredients used in the recipes in this book may contain nuts. Always check the
packaging before use.

Contents

The joys of baking

There's something extra special about a home-baked cake. While it may not have the perfectly proportioned features of a store-bought version, the flavor will almost certainly be far superior and you'll also know exactly what went into it! Home baking has never been so popular.

This book is the perfect choice for novice cooks who want to learn the basics of home baking, and it is also ideal for more experienced cooks, who will find a whole variety of new and original ideas to broaden their repertoire. There are over 140 recipes, ranging from cupcakes, muffins, and cookies to classic cakes, tarts, breads, pies, and desserts. Some of the recipes can easily be made in minutes, while others will take longer and require a little more skill and patience.

In the first few pages of the book, you'll find a comprehensive guide to all the essential information you need to start baking, including clear and concise details about basic ingredients, equipment, baking techniques, and methods.

This is followed by six bumper chapters filled with a range of inspirational recipes. Each one has clear and easy to understand numbered instructions and simple step-by-step pictures to guide you. The book is also full of useful hints and tips, from freezing information to time-saving techniques and flavor variations.

Secrets of successful baking

• Prepare the kitchen before you start by clearing work surfaces and making sure you have enough space to work in.

• Check that you have all the ingredients to make the recipe—there is nothing worse than running out of something at a crucial moment.

• Make sure that the cake pan is the correct size and prepare it by greasing and/or lining.

• Preheat the oven to the required temperature and take eggs out of the refrigerator one hour before starting. If the recipe requires softened butter, let it stand at room temperature for about an hour.

• For bread making, a warm kitchen will help the dough to rise, so turn the oven on earlier than needed.

• For pastry making, keep both your hands and equipment as cool as possible to prevent the fat from melting and making the pastry sticky.

There is nothing more satisfying than creating delicious, freshly baked homemade goodies for family and friends.

- Always measure ingredients carefully and use measuring spoons for leavening agents and flavorings.

- Don't be tempted to open the oven door too early—a blast of cold air can soon make a cake sink!

- To check if a sponge cake is ready, gently press the surface with your fingertips. It should spring back without leaving an impression. For deeper cakes or rich fruitcakes, check by inserting a toothpick into the center of the cake—it should come out clean.

- To check if bread is ready, hold the loaf with a thick dish towel and tap the bottom firmly with your knuckles—it should sound hollow.

- Let cakes and other baked goodies cool completely before storing in airtight plastic containers.

Essential baking ingredients

Whatever you choose to bake, the finest-quality ingredients will always give the best flavor. Here's a guide to some of the basics you'll need.

For the best results, always use eggs that have been left to reach room temperature for about an hour.

Flours

• White all-purpose flour is the most refined type of flour milled from soft wheat grains. It has a fine texture and is ideal for baking. Self-rising flour has added baking powder and salt. Whole-wheat flour is milled from the entire wheat grain and imparts a wonderful nutty flavor. It has a coarser texture than white flour and will absorb more liquid.

• Bread flour is milled from hard wheat, which has a higher gluten content than all-purpose flour, making it perfect for bread making. It can be mixed with flour with a low gluten content, such as rye or buckwheat, to produce a lighter textured loaf.

• Cornstarch is a fine white powder made from corn. Often used as a thickening agent, it can also be added to cakes, shortbread, and cookies to produce a light and crisp texture.

Fats

• Butter has a wonderful rich flavor and is nearly always the best choice for baking. Use unsalted for frostings and delicately flavored cakes.

Margarine can be used but its flavor is inferior and you won't get the same rich buttery taste. Low-fat margarines and spreads are not suitable for baking.

• Lard is a hard animal fat traditionally used in pastry making to produce a light and crisp texture. Flavorless vegetable shortening is a good alternative, suitable for vegetarians and healthier with no saturated fat.

• Oil is sometimes used in cake making and will produce a moist cake that will keep well. Use mild-flavored oils, such as sunflower.

Sugars and syrups

• Superfine sugar is ideal for baking because its fine grains dissolve easily. If it is difficult to get, process the same amount of granulated sugar in a food processor for about 60 seconds.

• Light and dark brown sugars have more depth of flavor than white sugars and add richness and color to your baking.

• Demerara sugar is a type of raw sugar with large golden crystals that add crunch and texture to crumb toppings or when sprinkled over the tops of cakes and cookies. Confectioners' sugar has a fine

powdery texture that dissolves easily, making it essential for icings and frostings.

• Corn syrup, dark molasses, honey, and maple syrup are all useful sweet syrups to keep in the pantry. They can be used in place of sugar in some recipes or for frostings and glazes.

Eggs

• Eggs are an indispensable baking ingredient. Always use fresh eggs at room temperature—they will beat to a larger volume. Make sure you check that you have the correct size for the recipe.

Leavening agents

• Baking powder, baking soda, and cream of tartar are all used as leavening agents to make cakes rise. Buy them in small quantities and check the expiration date before using, because they have a limited shelf life.

Flavorings

• Vanilla and almond extracts can provide a wonderful boost of flavor to cakes, cookies, and desserts. Be sure to buy natural extracts, not synthetic flavorings.

Dried fruits and nuts

• Dried fruits are vital ingredients in many baking recipes. They keep well stored in sealed plastic food bags or airtight containers but can quickly dry out if the packaging is left open. Candied fruit, such as cherries, should be rinsed and dried before use to remove their syrupy coating.

• Chopped nuts add flavor and texture to cakes and cookies and ground nuts add extra moistness. Because of their high oil content, nuts can quickly turn rancid, so buy in small quantities and store in a cool, dark place or freeze. Where possible, buy whole nuts and chop or grind just before using.

Chocolate

• Chocolate can vary considerably in quality and flavor. When buying dark chocolate, choose one that contains between 50 and 70 percent cocoa solids. Look for good-quality milk and white chocolates in the baking section of the supermarket.

Basic baking methods and techniques

Here are some of the basic methods and techniques that are essential to master when you want to become a regular baker.

For speed, use an electric mixer, or use a balloon whisk and a lot of elbow grease!

Creaming

Butter and sugar are beaten together thoroughly to form a light, pale, and fluffy mixture. It's essential that the butter is a soft, spreadable consistency before you start —but not melted.

Use a wooden spoon or an electric mixer on a low speed and be careful not to overbeat, or the mixture will become oily.

Adding eggs

Always beat the eggs before gradually adding them to the creamed mixture.

Beat well after each addition and, if the mixture begins to curdle, add a couple of spoonfuls of measured flour before adding more eggs.

Folding in

Sift the dry ingredients and use a large metal spoon to gently cut and fold it through the creamed mixture.

Don't use a wooden spoon or beat the mixture, because this will knock out air bubbles and produce a dense cake.

Rubbing in

This technique is used for pastries, biscuits, and some cakes. The fat needs to be chilled and diced or grated. Make sure your hands are clean and cold and rub the fat into flour between the tips of your fingers until it resembles fine bread crumbs.

Occasionally shake the bowl to bring any large lumps of fat to the surface.

Beating

To make meringues or sponge cakes, large amounts of air need to be incorporated into the cake batter or egg whites.

For speed, use an electric mixer, or use a large balloon whisk and plenty of elbow grease!

Baking blind

This term refers to a technique to partly or completely bake a pastry shell before adding a filling.

Line the pastry shell with a circle of parchment paper and weigh it down with ceramic pie weights or dried breans—this prevents the pastry from rising.

Kneading

The stretching, folding, and pushing of bread dough with floured hands is a vital technique that strengthens the dough and makes it more elastic. This, in turn, helps the dough to rise.

It will take 5–10 minutes of kneading to achieve a smooth and elastic dough.

Melting chocolate

Break chocolate into pieces and place in a clean, heatproof bowl. Sit the bowl over a saucepan of barely simmering water—do not let the bottom of the bowl touch the water or the chocolate will burn—and heat until the chocolate has just melted.

Be careful to avoid drips of water or condensation from getting into the bowl, becuase this will cause the chocolate to "seize" and become grainy.

Frosting

To frost cakes, first use a large rubber spatula to apply a thin layer of frosting all over the cake to secure loose crumbs and fill any gaps and cracks.

Then spread a thicker layer over the top and sides, swirling the frosting with the tip of the spatula.

Piping

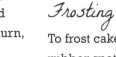

To pipe frostings or cream fillings, use a large pastry bag fitted with a plain or fluted tip. Twist the top of the bag to enclose the filling and hold and squeeze the bag firmly with one hand.

Essential baking equipment

It is worth buying good-quality equipment that will last a long time—if you like baking cupcakes, then invest in a good muffin pan. If you make layer cakes only occasionally, it is probably best to borrow cake pans from a friend.

Other electrical equipment that can make life easier in the kitchen, but not essential, include a food processor, blender, and a mini chopper.

Cake pans

Although they are not cheap, stainless steel pans are durable, distribute heat evenly, and won't warp. Heavy duty nonstick pans are great for inverting cakes with ease. Flexible silicone bakeware is also now popular and is easy to use, clean, and store. Wash pans or silicone bakeware in warm soapy water and make sure they are completely dry before storing.

You can slowly build up your collection of bakeware, but a basic collection should include:

- Deep round and square cake pans, 8–9 inches
- Two standard, shallow 8-inch round cake pans
- Two large baking sheets
- Round springform pan, 8–9 inches
- Loaf pans, 8½ inches and 9 inches
- 12-cup muffin pan
- Loose-bottom tart pan, 8–9 inches
- Rectangular, shallow sheet pan

Greasing and lining cake pans

Always follow the recipe instructions about preparing pans. Grease pans with melted or softened butter or a flavorless vegetable oil. If a pan needs to be greased and floured, sprinkle a little flour in the pan, then tilt and tap it firmly, until the flour coats the bottom and sides evenly. Tip out any excess flour.

Electric mixer

Not an absolute essential but certainly worth buying if you plan to do a lot of baking. A handheld one with at least three speed settings will give you plenty of control. An immersion blender can be used for whipping things in a saucepan. If you do get serious about baking, a stand mixer might be worth the investment.

Mixing bowls

A selection of three to four bowls in different sizes is essential. Toughened and heatproof glass bowls, such as Pyrex, are ideal.

Measuring spoons and cups

A set of standard kitchen measuring spoons and cups will cost little but will provide accurate measurements. Use a leveled spoon or cup unless stated otherwise. A heatproof glass measuring cup with clear markings on the side will make measuring liquids easy—check the marks at eye level for accuracy.

Sifters and strainers

Use a sifter with a trigger-style handle for breaking up lumps in dry ingredients, or choose rustproof metal or nylon strainers with a fine mesh. After washing metal sifters and strainers, dry thoroughly before storing them.

Spoons and spatulas

Buy a set of different-size wooden spoons for creaming and mixing. Always dry them thoroughly after washing and throw away any that are old or split. A good-size metal spoon is essential for folding in and flexible silicone spatulas are handy for light mixing of ingredients and scraping mixture from bowls.

Other essentials

- Good set of chef's knives
- Rolling pin
- Pastry brushes
- Cookie cutters
- Grater
- Large pastry bag and tips
- Citrus squeezer
- Balloon whisk
- Wire rack for cooling

A note about ovens and timings

Ovens can vary considerably, depending on whether they are gas, electric, or convection, so always use the oven temperature in the recipe as a guide. If your oven runs a little hot or cold, then adjust the temperature accordingly. It's worth investing in an oven thermometer for complete accuracy. Convection ovens tend to cook more quickly than conventional ovens, so you need to reduce the temperature by about 68°F or follow the manufacturers' guide.

Classic Chocolate Cake *18*

Frosted Fruits Cake *20*

Coffee Bundt Cake *22*

Red Velvet Cake *24*

Lemon & Blueberry Cornmeal Cake *26*

Strawberry Layer Cake *28*

Chocolate & Sour Cherry Cake *30*

White Chocolate Coffee Cake *32*

Iced Pound Cake *34*

Apple Crumb Cake *36*

Devil's Food Cake *38*

Pumpkin Spice Cake *40*

Mocha Cake *42*

Glazed Gingerbread *44*

Coconut Layer Cake *46*

Boston Cream Pie *48*

Pineapple & Coconut Cake *50*

Angel Food Cake *52*

Chocolate Flake Cake *54*

Cinnamon & Walnut Layer Cake *56*

Rich Fruitcake *58*

Grasshopper Cake *60*

Maple & Pecan Bundt Cake *62*

Coffee & Walnut Cake *64*

Cakes

Classic Chocolate Cake

 SERVES 10    PREP TIME: 40 minutes plus chilling    COOKING TIME: 25–30 minutes

nutritional information per serving	581 cal, 41g fat, 25g sat fat, 32g total sugars, 0.7g salt

For sheer indulgence, nothing beats a slice of moist chocolate cake smothered in a rich and creamy frosting.

INGREDIENTS

⅔ cup unsweetened cocoa powder

½ cup boiling water

1¾ sticks salted butter, softened, plus extra for greasing

⅔ cup superfine sugar

⅓ cup firmly packed light brown sugar

4 eggs, beaten

1 teaspoon vanilla extract

1⅔ cups all-purpose flour

2¼ teaspoons baking powder

frosting

7 ounces semisweet chocolate, broken into pieces

1 stick unsalted butter

½ cup heavy cream

1. Preheat the oven to 350°F. Grease two 8-inch cake pans and line with parchment paper.

2. Blend the cocoa powder and water to a smooth paste and set aside. Put the butter, superfine sugar, and brown sugar into a large bowl and beat together until pale and creamy. Gradually beat in the eggs, then stir in the cocoa paste and vanilla extract.

3. Sift in the flour and baking powder and fold in gently. Divide the batter between the prepared pans. Bake in the preheated oven for 25–30 minutes, or until risen and just springy to the touch. Let cool in the pans for 5 minutes, then invert onto a wire rack to cool completely.

4. To make the frosting, put the chocolate and butter into a heatproof bowl set over a saucepan of simmering water and heat until melted. Remove from the heat and stir in the cream. Let cool for 20 minutes, then chill in the refrigerator for 40–50 minutes, stirring occasionally, until thick enough to spread.

5. Sandwich the sponges together with one-third of the frosting, then spread the remainder over the top and sides of the cake.

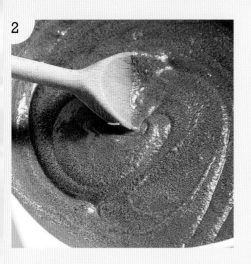

2

3

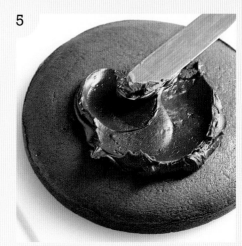

5

Frosted Fruits Cake

 SERVES 16

 PREP TIME:
1 hour
plus chilling

 COOKING TIME:
35–40 minutes

nutritional information per serving	502 cal, 33g fat, 20g sat fat, 35g total sugars, 0.6g salt

This impressive cake is perfect for a summer afternoon get together or as a dessert after a leisurely lunch. Use firm, undamaged fruit so their juices don't seep into the frosting.

INGREDIENTS

2½ sticks salted butter, softened, plus extra for greasing

2⅓ cups superfine sugar

5 eggs, beaten

1 tablespoon vanilla extract

2¼ cups all-purpose flour

1 tablespoon baking powder

3 tablespoons milk

⅓ cup raspberry preserves or strawberry preserves

⅔ cup heavy cream

about 3 cups mixed berries, such as strawberries, raspberries, and blueberries

confectioners' sugar, for sprinkling

frosting

1 cup cream cheese

1 stick unsalted butter, softened

1 teaspoon lemon juice

1 cup confectioners' sugar

pink food coloring

1. Preheat the oven to 350°F. Grease two 8-inch cake pans and line with parchment paper. Put the butter and superfine sugar into a bowl and beat together until pale and creamy. Gradually beat in the eggs, then stir in the vanilla extract. Sift in the flour and baking powder and fold in gently. Stir in the milk. Divide the batter between the prepared pans. Bake in the preheated oven for 35–40 minutes, or until springy to the touch. Invert onto a wire rack to cool.

2. Place one of the cakes on a flat serving plate and spread with the preserves. Whip the cream until it is just holding its shape. Spread the cream over the preserves, almost to the edges of the cake. Position the second cake on top and press down gently so the cream is level with the edges of the cake.

3. To make the frosting, beat together the cream cheese and butter. Add the lemon juice and confectioners' sugar and beat until light and creamy. Beat a dash of pink food coloring into the frosting to color it the palest shade of pink. Using a spatula, spread a thin layer over the top and sides of the cake to seal in the crumbs. The cake will still show through at this stage, but it will be covered by the second layer of frosting. Chill in the refrigerator for 15 minutes.

4. Use the spatula to spread a thicker layer of frosting around the sides of the cake. Spread the remainder over the top. Once evenly covered, use the edge of the spatula to swirl the frosting as smoothly or as textured as you desire. Arrange the fruits on top of the cake. Put a little confectioners' sugar in a small, fine strainer and gently tap it over the fruits to lightly frost.

3

4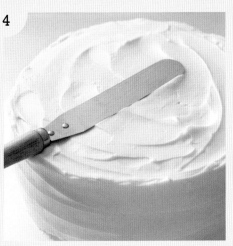

4

Coffee Bundt Cake

 SERVES 14

 PREP TIME:
50 minutes
plus cooling

 COOKING TIME:
50 minutes

nutritional information per serving	505 cal, 28g fat, 17g sat fat, 36g total sugars, 0.9g salt

Bundt cakes cook quickly and, therefore, stay deliciously moist, because of the hole through the center of the pan.

INGREDIENTS

3¼ cups all-purpose flour, plus extra for dusting

1 tablespoon baking powder

1 teaspoon baking soda

3 tablespoons espresso coffee powder

2½ sticks salted butter, softened, plus extra for greasing

½ cup firmly packed light brown sugar

1 cup maple syrup

3 eggs, beaten

1 cup buttermilk

1 cup heavy cream

decoration

¼ cup maple syrup

1⅔ cups confectioners' sugar

1 tablespoon unsalted butter, melted

20 chocolate-coated coffee beans

1. Preheat the oven to 350°F. Grease and lightly flour a 3-quart Bundt pan.

2. Sift the flour, baking powder, baking soda, and coffee powder into a bowl. In a separate bowl, beat together the butter and brown sugar until pale and creamy. Gradually beat in the maple syrup. Beat in the eggs slowly, adding 3 tablespoons of the flour mixture to prevent it from curdling.

3. Mix together the buttermilk and cream and add half to the butter mixture. Sprinkle in half of the flour mixture and fold together gently. Add the remaining buttermilk and flour mixtures and mix together gently until just combined.

4. Spoon the batter into the prepared pan and smooth the surface. Bake in the preheated oven for about 50 minutes, or until well risen and a toothpick inserted into the center comes out clean. Let stand in the pan for 10 minutes, then loosen with a knife and invert onto a wire rack to cool completely.

5. To decorate, beat the maple syrup in a bowl with 1¼ cups of the confectioners' sugar and the butter, until smooth and thickly coating the back of a wooden spoon. Transfer the cake to a serving plate and spoon the icing around the top of the cake so it starts to run down the sides.

6. Beat the remaining confectioners' sugar in a small bowl with 1½–2 teaspoons of water to make a smooth paste. Using a teaspoon, drizzle the icing over the cake. Spread the coffee beans over the top.

2

5

6

Red Velvet Cake

 SERVES 12    PREP TIME: 20 minutes plus cooling    COOKING TIME: 25–30 minutes

nutritional information per serving	510 cal, 32g fat, 20g sat fat, 28g total sugars, 0.5g salt

A popular cake with a rich buttermilk-flavored chocolate sponge, it is colored deep red by edible food coloring and topped off with a traditional vanilla cream cheese frosting.

INGREDIENTS

2 sticks unsalted butter, plus extra for greasing
¼ cup water
⅔ cup unsweetened cocoa powder
3 eggs, beaten
1 cup buttermilk
2 teaspoons vanilla extract
2 tablespoons red edible food coloring
2¼ cups all-purpose flour
½ cup cornstarch
1½ teaspoons baking powder
1⅓ cups superfine sugar

frosting
1 cup cream cheese
3 tablespoons unsalted butter
3 tablespoons superfine sugar
1 teaspoon vanilla extract

1. Preheat the oven to 375°F. Grease two 9-inch cake pans and line with parchment paper.

2. Place the butter, water, and cocoa powder in a small saucepan and heat gently, without boiling, stirring until melted and smooth. Remove from the heat and let cool slightly.

3. Beat together the eggs, buttermilk, vanilla extract, and food coloring in a bowl until frothy. Beat in the butter mixture. Sift together the flour, cornstarch, and baking powder, then stir quickly and evenly into the mixture with the superfine sugar.

4. Divide the batter between the prepared pans and bake in the preheated oven for 25–30 minutes, or until risen and firm to the touch. Let cool in the pans for 3–4 minutes, then invert onto a wire rack to cool completely.

5. To make the frosting, beat together all the ingredients until smooth. Use about half of the frosting to sandwich together the cakes, then spread the remainder over the top, swirling with a spatula.

Lemon & Blueberry Cornmeal Cake

 SERVES 8    PREP TIME: 15 minutes plus cooling    COOKING TIME: 40–45 minutes

nutritional information per serving	388 cal, 25g fat, 10g sat fat, 21g total sugars, 0.5g salt

Cornmeal is used in place of flour in this cake, giving it a wonderful texture and vibrant color.

INGREDIENTS

1 stick salted butter, softened, plus extra for greasing

¾ cup superfine sugar

finely grated rind of 1 lemon, plus 2 tablespoons juice

3 eggs, beaten

¾ cup cornmeal

1¼ cups almond meal (ground almonds)

1 teaspoon baking powder

¼ cup Greek-style yogurt

¾ cup fresh or frozen blueberries

confectioners' sugar, for dusting

1. Preheat the oven to 350°F. Grease an 8-inch round springform cake pan and line with parchment paper.

2. Put the butter, superfine sugar, lemon rind, and lemon juice into a large bowl and beat together until pale and fluffy. Gradually beat in the eggs, then stir in the cornmeal, almond meal, baking powder, and yogurt.

3. Fold in two-thirds of the blueberries. Spoon the batter into the prepared pan, smooth the surface, and sprinkle with the remaining blueberries.

4. Bake in the preheated oven for 40–45 minutes, or until just firm and deep golden around the edges. Let cool in the pan for 20 minutes, then unclip the pan and carefully transfer the cake to a wire rack. Serve warm or cold, dusted with confectioners' sugar.

2

3

4

GOES WELL WITH
This cake is delicious served warm with crème fraîche or whipped cream and extra berries.

Strawberry Layer Cake

 SERVES 8

 PREP TIME:
30 minutes
plus cooling

 COOKING TIME:
25–30 minutes

nutritional information per serving	566 cal, 42g fat, 25g sat fat, 28g total sugars, 0.8g salt

This classic layer cake is given the star treatment with a luxurious filling of preserves, softly whipped cream, and fresh strawberries. Just perfect for a summer afternoon coffee break.

INGREDIENTS

1⅓ cups all-purpose flour

2¾ teaspoons baking powder

1½ sticks salted butter, softened, plus extra for greasing

1 cup superfine sugar

3 eggs, beaten

confectioners' sugar, for dusting

filling

3 tablespoons raspberry preserves

1¼ cups heavy cream, whipped

16 fresh strawberries, halved

1. Preheat the oven to 350°F. Grease two 8-inch cake pans and line with parchment paper.

2. Sift the flour and baking powder into a bowl and add the butter, sugar, and eggs. Mix together, then beat well until smooth.

3. Divide the batter evenly between the prepared pans and smooth the surfaces. Bake in the preheated oven for 25–30 minutes, or until well risen and golden brown, and the cakes feel springy when lightly pressed.

4. Let cool in the pans for 5 minutes, then invert and peel off the parchment paper. Transfer to wire racks to cool completely. Sandwich the cakes together with the raspberry preserves, whipped cream, and strawberry halves. Dust with confectioners' sugar.

2

3

4

COOK'S NOTE
To create a lacy pattern, place a doily over the cake and dust with confectioners' sugar.

Chocolate & Sour Cherry Cake

 SERVES 12

 PREP TIME: 30 minutes plus chilling

 COOKING TIME: 40–45 minutes

nutritional information per serving	430 cal, 28g fat, 15g sat fat, 32g total sugars, 0.3g salt

An intensely dark and rich chocolate cake with a rum-flavored chocolate frosting, this is definitely one for the grown-ups. Serve with a spoon of crème fraîche or whipped cream.

INGREDIENTS

6 ounces bittersweet chocolate, broken into pieces

1 stick salted butter, diced, plus extra for greasing

3 extra-large eggs, separated

½ cup dark brown sugar

1 cup all-purpose flour

1½ teaspoons baking powder

½ cup almond meal (ground almonds)

½ cup chopped dried cherries

chocolate curls, unsweetened cocoa powder, and fresh cherries, to decorate (optional)

frosting

6 ounces bittersweet chocolate, broken into pieces

⅓ cup heavy cream

4 tablespoons unsalted butter

1 tablespoon rum

1. Preheat the oven to 350°F. Grease an 8-inch round cake pan and line with parchment paper.

2. Place the chocolate and butter in a large heatproof bowl set over a saucepan of simmering water and heat until melted. Remove from the heat and stir until smooth. Cool for 10 minutes, stirring occasionally.

3. Place the egg yolks and sugar in a large bowl and, using an electric handheld mixer, beat until pale and creamy. Add the melted chocolate and beat until thoroughly combined. Sift in the flour and baking powder, then stir in the almond meal and dried cherries.

4. In a separate bowl, beat the egg whites until soft peaks form, then gently fold into the chocolate mixture. Spoon into the prepared pan and gently smooth the surface.

5. Bake in the preheated oven for 40–45 minutes, or until just firm to the touch and a toothpick inserted into the center comes out clean. Cool in the pan for 10 minutes, then invert onto a wire rack to cool completely.

6. For the frosting, place the chocolate, cream, and butter in a heatproof bowl set over a saucepan of simmering water. Heat until melted, then remove from the heat and beat in the rum. Cool for 20 minutes, then chill in the refrigerator, stirring occasionally, for about 30 minutes, or until thick enough to spread.

7. Spread the frosting over the top of the cake. If using, decorate with chocolate curls, dust lightly with cocoa powder, and top with the cherries.

2

5

7

White Chocolate Coffee Cake

 SERVES 10   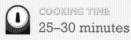 PREP TIME: 30 minutes plus chilling    COOKING TIME: 25–30 minutes

nutritional information per serving	467 cal, 27g fat, 16g sat fat, 40g total sugars, 0.2g salt

This coffee-flavored cake has a wonderful smooth and tangy crème fraîche and white chocolate frosting.

INGREDIENTS

3 tablespoons unsalted butter, plus extra for greasing

3 ounces white chocolate, broken into pieces

⅔ cup superfine sugar

4 extra-large eggs, beaten

2 tablespoons strong black coffee

1 teaspoon vanilla extract

1 cup all-purpose flour

frosting

6 ounces white chocolate

6 tablespoons unsalted butter

½ cup crème fraîche

1 cup confectioners' sugar, sifted

1 tablespoon coffee liqueur

1. Preheat the oven to 350°F. Grease two 8-inch cake pans and line with parchment paper. Place the butter and chocolate in a bowl set over a saucepan of hot water on low heat until just melted. Stir to mix, then remove from the heat. Place the superfine sugar, eggs, coffee, and vanilla in a bowl set over a saucepan of hot water and beat until it leaves a trail when the beaters or whisk are lifted.

2. Remove from the heat, sift in the flour, and mix in lightly and evenly. Quickly stir in the butter-and-chocolate mixture, then divide the batter between the prepared pans. Bake in the preheated oven for 25–30 minutes, until risen, golden brown, and springy to the touch. Let cool in the pans for 2 minutes, then invert onto a wire rack.

3. To make the frosting, put the chocolate and butter into a bowl set over a saucepan of hot water and heat gently until melted. Remove from the heat, stir in the crème fraîche, add the confectioners' sugar and coffee liqueur, and mix. Chill until thick. Sandwich the cakes together with a third of the frosting, then spread the rest over the cake.

1

2

3

COOK'S NOTE
Be careful when melting white chocolate because it can turn grainy if overheated.

Iced Pound Cake

 SERVES 10    PREP TIME: 30 minutes plus cooling    COOKING TIME: 1–1¼ hours

nutritional information per serving	388 cal, 17.5g fat, 10.5g sat fat, 36g total sugars, 0.2g salt

This cake has a firm texture with a buttery flavor that is made sweeter with a lemon icing.

INGREDIENTS

1½ sticks unsalted butter, softened, plus extra for greasing
1 cup superfine sugar
finely grated rind of 1 lemon
3 eggs, lightly beaten
2 cups all-purpose flour
2 teaspoons baking powder
2 tablespoons milk
1 tablespoon lemon juice

icing

1⅓ cups confectioners' sugar
2–3 tablespoons lemon juice
2 teaspoons lemon curd, warmed

1. Preheat the oven to 325°F. Grease a 9-inch loaf pan and line with parchment paper.

2. Place the butter and superfine sugar in a large bowl and beat together until pale and creamy. Beat in the lemon rind, then gradually beat in the eggs. Sift the flour and baking powder into the mixture and fold in gently until thoroughly incorporated. Fold in the milk and lemon juice.

3. Spoon the batter into the prepared pan and bake in the preheated oven for 1–1¼ hours, or until well risen, golden brown, and a toothpick inserted into the center comes out clean. Cool in the pan for 15 minutes, then invert onto a wire rack to cool completely.

4. For the icing, sift the confectioners' sugar into a bowl. Add the lemon juice and stir to make a smooth, thick icing. Gently spread the icing over the top of the cake. Drizzle the warmed lemon curd over the icing and drag a toothpick through the icing to create a swirled effect.

2

3

4

COOK'S NOTE
Cover the top of
the cake with
aluminum foil
after 50 minutes
to prevent it from
overbrowning.

Apple Crumb Cake

 SERVES 10    PREP TIME: 30 minutes plus cooling   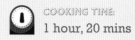 COOKING TIME: 1 hour, 20 mins

nutritional information per serving	451 cal, 26g fat, 13g sat fat, 28g total sugars, 0.7g salt

Chunks of moist apple in a spiced sponge, topped off with a deliciously nutty crumb crust—irresistible!

INGREDIENTS

1½ sticks salted butter, softened, plus extra for greasing

1 cup superfine sugar

3 extra-large eggs, beaten

2 tablespoons milk

1¾ cups all-purpose flour

2½ teaspoons baking powder

1 teaspoon ground cinnamon

½ teaspoon grated nutmeg

2 cooking apples (1 pound), such as Granny Smith or Pippin, peeled, cored, and chopped

ice cream or crème fraîche, to serve

crumb topping

¾ cup all-purpose flour

4 tablespoons salted butter, chilled and diced

¼ cup demerara sugar or other raw sugar

⅓ cup blanched hazelnuts, chopped

1. Preheat the oven to 350°F. Grease a 9-inch round springform cake pan and line with parchment paper.

2. Put the butter and superfine sugar into a large bowl and beat together until pale and fluffy, then gradually beat in the eggs. Stir in the milk. Sift together the flour, baking powder, and spices and gently fold in until thoroughly incorporated.

3. Spoon half the batter into the prepared pan and spread half the apples over the batter. Spoon over the remaining batter and spread evenly. Top with the remaining apples.

4. To make the crumb topping, sift the flour into a bowl, then add the butter and rub in until the mixture resembles bread crumbs. Stir in the demerara sugar and nuts. Sprinkle the mixture evenly over the top of the cake.

5. Bake in the preheated oven for 1 hour, then cover loosely with aluminum foil to prevent the cake from overbrowning. Cook for an additional 10–20 minutes, or until golden brown and firm to the touch. Let cool in the pan for 20 minutes, then unclip the pan and carefully transfer to a wire rack. Serve warm or cold, with ice cream.

Devil's Food Cake

 SERVES 10

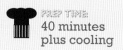 PREP TIME:
40 minutes
plus cooling

 COOKING TIME:
35–40 minutes

nutritional information per serving	583 cal, 32g fat, 20g sat fat, 52g total sugars, 0.6g salt

This classic cake has a moist and dark chocolate sponge smothered in a rich and creamy chocolate frosting. It is a great cake to serve for a birthday celebration because it can be made in advance and is easy to slice!

INGREDIENTS

5 ounces semisweet chocolate, broken into pieces

½ cup whole milk

2 tablespoons unsweetened cocoa powder

1¼ sticks unsalted butter, softened, plus extra for greasing

⅔ cup firmly packed light brown sugar

3 eggs, separated

¼ cup sour cream or crème fraîche

1⅔ cups all-purpose flour

1 teaspoon baking soda

frosting

5 ounces semisweet chocolate

½ cup unsweetened cocoa powder

¼ cup sour cream or crème fraîche

1 tablespoon corn syrup

3 tablespoons unsalted butter

¼ cup water

1⅔ cups confectioners' sugar

1. Preheat the oven to 325°F. Grease and line two 8-inch cake pans.

2. Place the chocolate, milk, and cocoa powder in a heatproof bowl set over a saucepan of simmering water, and heat gently, stirring, until melted and smooth. Remove from the heat.

3. In a large bowl, beat together the butter and brown sugar until pale and creamy. Beat in the egg yolks, then the sour cream and the melted chocolate mixture. Sift in the flour and baking soda, then fold in evenly. In a separate, clean bowl, beat the egg whites until stiff enough to hold firm peaks. Fold into the mixture lightly.

4. Divide the batter between the prepared cake pans, smooth the surfaces, and bake in the preheated oven for 35–40 minutes, or until risen and firm to the touch. Cool in the pans for 10 minutes, then invert onto a wire rack to cool completely.

5. To make the frosting, place the chocolate, cocoa powder, sour cream, corn syrup, butter, and water in a saucepan and heat gently, until melted. Remove from the heat and sift in the confectioners' sugar, stirring until smooth. Cool, stirring occasionally, until the mixture begins to thicken and hold its shape.

6. Slice the cakes in half horizontally with a sharp knife to make four layers. Sandwich together the cakes with about one-third of the frosting. Spread the remainder over the top and sides of the cakes, swirling with a spatula.

Pumpkin Spice Cake

 SERVES 8

 PREP TIME:
25 minutes
plus cooling

 COOKING TIME:
35–40 minutes

nutritional information per serving	631 cal, 39g fat, 12g sat fat, 44g total sugars, 0.9g salt

This lightly spiced fruit and nut cake is smothered with a rich and creamy maple syrup frosting.

INGREDIENTS

¾ cup sunflower oil,
plus extra for greasing
¾ cup packed light brown sugar
3 eggs, beaten
1 cup canned pumpkin puree
⅔ cup raisins
grated rind of 1 orange
⅔ cup walnut pieces
1¾ cups all-purpose flour
1 teaspoon baking soda
2¾ teaspoons baking powder
2 teaspoons allspice

frosting
1 cup mascarpone cheese
⅔ cup confectioners' sugar
3 tablespoons maple syrup

1. Preheat the oven to 350°F. Grease a 9-inch square cake pan and line with parchment paper.

2. In a large bowl, beat together the oil, brown sugar, and eggs. Stir in the pumpkin puree, raisins, orange rind, and ½ cup of the walnut pieces.

3. Sift together the flour, baking soda, baking powder, and allspice and fold into the pumpkin mixture. Spoon the batter into the prepared pan and bake in the preheated oven for 35–40 minutes, or until golden brown and firm to the touch. Let cool in the pan for 5 minutes, then invert onto a wire rack to cool completely.

4. To make the frosting, put the mascarpone cheese, confectioners' sugar, and maple syrup into a bowl and beat together until smooth. Spread over the top of the cake, swirling with a spatula. Finely chop the remaining walnut pieces and sprinkle over the top of the cake.

2

3

4

HEALTHY HINT
For a lighter frosting, use thick Greek-style yogurt sweetened to taste with honey. Spread over the cake just before serving.

Mocha Cake

 SERVES 12  PREP TIME: 40 minutes plus cooling  COOKING TIME: 25–30 minutes

nutritional information per serving	532 cal, 37g fat, 22g sat fat, 32g total sugars, 0.8g salt

This delicious cake is the perfect combination of two classic flavors—chocolate and coffee.

INGREDIENTS

1¾ cups all-purpose flour

3¾ teaspoons baking powder

2 tablespoons unsweetened cocoa powder

2 sticks salted butter, softened, plus extra for greasing

1 cup firmly packed light brown sugar

4 extra-large eggs, beaten

4 ounces semisweet chocolate, melted

2 tablespoons superfine sugar

3 tablespoons strong black coffee

frosting

6 tablespoons unsalted butter, softened

1 cup mascarpone cheese

½ cup confectioners' sugar

2 tablespoons strong black coffee

unsweetened cocoa powder, to dust

chocolate-coated coffee beans, to decorate

1. Preheat the oven to 350°F. Grease two 8-inch cake pans and line with parchment paper.

2. Sift together the flour, baking powder, and cocoa powder into a large bowl. Add the butter, brown sugar, and eggs and, using an electric handheld mixer, beat together for 3–4 minutes, or until the mixture is smooth and creamy. Fold in the melted chocolate.

3. Divide the batter between the prepared cake pans and bake in the preheated oven for 25–30 minutes, or until risen and firm to the touch.

4. Place the superfine sugar and black coffee in a small saucepan and heat gently for 1–2 minutes. Cool for 10 minutes. Pierce the tops of the warm cakes all over with a toothpick and spoon the coffee syrup over the cakes. Let the cakes cool in the pans.

5. To make the frosting, place the butter and mascarpone cheese in a bowl and beat together until well blended. Beat in the confectioners' sugar and coffee until smooth.

6. Remove the cakes from the pans and sandwich together with half the frosting. Swirl the remaining frosting over the top of the cake. Dust with cocoa powder and decorate with chocolate-coated coffee beans.

2

3

6

Glazed Gingerbread

 SERVES 12

 PREP TIME: 30 minutes plus cooling

 COOKING TIME: 1–1¼ hours

nutritional information per serving	300 cal, 10g fat, 6g sat fat, 34g total sugars, 0.6g salt

The flavor of this cake will improve with time. If you have the patience, wrap the cake in wax paper and store in a cool place for a few days before icing.

INGREDIENTS

2 cups all-purpose flour

1 teaspoon baking soda

1½ teaspoons ground ginger

1 teaspoon ground allspice

1 stick salted butter, plus extra for greasing

½ cup firmly packed light brown sugar

⅔ cup corn syrup

¼ cup dark molasses

2 extra-large eggs, beaten

2 tablespoons milk

icing

1 cup confectioners' sugar

1 tablespoon preserved ginger syrup

1–2 tablespoons water

1 piece preserved ginger, finely chopped

1. Preheat the oven to 325°F. Grease a 7-inch square cake pan and line with parchment paper.

2. Sift the flour, baking soda, ground ginger, and allspice into a large bowl. Place the butter, brown sugar, corn syrup, and molasses in a saucepan and heat gently, stirring all the time, until the butter has melted. Cool for 5 minutes.

3. Stir the melted mixture into the bowl and mix well. Add the eggs and milk and beat until thoroughly incorporated.

4. Spoon the batter into the prepared pan and bake in the preheated oven for 1–1¼ hours, or until well risen and firm to the touch. Cool in the pan for 15 minutes, then invert onto a wire rack to cool completely.

5. To make the icing, sift the confectioners' sugar into a bowl. Stir in the ginger syrup and enough of the water to make a smooth icing that just coats the back of a wooden spoon.

6. Spoon the icing over the top of the cake, letting it run down the sides. Sprinkle with the preserved ginger and let set.

2

4

6

Coconut Layer Cake

 SERVES 8

 PREP TIME:
40 minutes
plus cooling

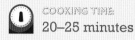 COOKING TIME:
20–25 minutes

nutritional information per serving	592 cal, 42g fat, 26g sat fat, 28g total sugars, 0.35g salt

This cake is perfect for a special occasion with light-as-air coconut sponge filled and covered with a divinely creamy, smooth frosting.

INGREDIENTS

6 extra-large eggs, beaten

¾ cup plus 2 tablespoons superfine sugar

1⅓ cup plus 1 tablespoon all-purpose flour

1 cup dry unsweetened coconut

4 tablespoons salted butter, melted and cooled, plus extra for greasing

toasted coconut shavings, to decorate

frosting
1 cup mascarpone cheese

¼ cup coconut milk

2 tablespoons superfine sugar

⅔ cup heavy cream

1. Preheat the oven to 350°F. Grease three 8-inch round cake pans and line with parchment paper.

2. Put the eggs and sugar into a large, heatproof bowl set over a saucepan of simmering water. Beat with an electric handheld mixer until the mixture is thick and pale and leaves a trail when the beaters are lifted.

3. Sift half of the flour over the beaten mixture and gently fold in, then sift the rest of the flour over the mixture and fold in again. Fold in the coconut. Pour the butter in a thin stream over the mixture and fold in until just incorporated.

4. Divide the batter between the prepared pans and bake in the preheated oven for 20–25 minutes, or until light golden and springy to the touch. Let cool in the pans for 5 minutes, then invert onto a wire rack to cool completely.

5. To make the frosting, put the mascarpone cheese, coconut milk, and sugar into a bowl and beat together until smooth. Whip the cream until it holds soft peaks, then fold it into the mixture.

6. Sandwich the sponges together with one-third of the frosting and spread the remainder over the top and sides of the cake. Decorate with coconut shavings.

2

4

6

Boston Cream Pie

 SERVES 10    PREP TIME: 40 minutes plus cooling    COOKING TIME: 20–25 minutes

nutritional information per serving	468 cal, 31g fat, 18g sat fat, 27g total sugars, 0.3g salt

Not a pie but an indulgent combination of two light sponge cakes, sandwiched with a rich vanilla pastry cream and topped with a glossy chocolate glaze.

INGREDIENTS

4 extra-large eggs, beaten

½ cup plus 1 tablespoon superfine sugar

1 cup all-purpose flour

3 tablespoons salted butter, melted and cooled, plus extra for greasing

pastry cream
2 eggs

¼ cup superfine sugar

1 teaspoon vanilla extract

2 tablespoons all-purpose flour

2 tablespoons cornstarch

1¼ cups milk

⅔ cup heavy cream, softly whipped

chocolate glaze
4 ounces semisweet chocolate, grated

1 tablespoon corn syrup

2 tablespoons salted butter

⅔ cup heavy cream

1. Preheat the oven to 350°F. Grease two 9-inch cake pans and line with parchment paper.

2. Place the eggs and sugar in a heatproof bowl set over a saucepan of simmering water. Using an electric handheld mixer, beat together until the mixture is thick and pale and leaves a trail when the beaters are lifted.

3. Sift the flour over the beaten mixture and fold in gently. Pour the butter in a thin stream over the mixture and fold in until just incorporated. Divide the batter between the prepared pans and bake in the preheated oven for 20–25 minutes, or until light golden and springy to the touch. Cool in the pans for 5 minutes, then invert onto a wire rack to cool completely.

4. For the pastry cream, beat together the eggs, sugar, and vanilla extract. Blend the flour and cornstarch to a paste with ¼ cup of the milk, then beat into the egg mixture. Heat the remaining milk until almost boiling and pour onto the egg mixture, stirring all the time. Return to the saucepan and cook over low heat, beating all the time, until smooth and thickened. Pour into a bowl and cover with dampened wax paper. Let stand until cold, then fold in the whipped cream.

5. For the glaze, place the chocolate, corn syrup, and butter in a heatproof bowl. Heat the cream until almost boiling, then pour over the chocolate. Let stand for 1 minute, then stir until smooth.

6. To assemble, sandwich the sponges together with the pastry cream. Spread the chocolate glaze over the top of the cake.

3

4

5

Pineapple & Coconut Cake

 SERVES 12

 PREP TIME:
30 minutes
plus cooling

 COOKING TIME:
25 minutes

nutritional information
per serving　　377 cal, 19g fat, 12g sat fat, 34g total sugars, 0.4g salt

A tube cake always looks impressive and is easy to slice and serve. Pineapple and coconut give this one a truly tropical flavor.

INGREDIENTS

1 (15½-ounce) can pineapple slices, drained

1 stick unsalted butter, softened, plus extra for greasing

1 cup superfine sugar

2 eggs and 1 egg yolk, beaten

1¾ cups all-purpose flour, plus extra for dusting

1 teaspoon baking powder

½ teaspoon baking soda

½ cup dry unsweetened coconut

frosting

¾ cup cream cheese

1⅓ cups confectioners' sugar

1. Preheat the oven to 350°F. Grease and lightly flour a 9-inch tube pan. Place the pineapple rings in a blender or food processor and process briefly until just crushed.

2. Beat together the butter and superfine sugar until light and fluffy. Gradually beat in the eggs until combined. Sift together the flour, baking powder, and baking soda over the egg mixture and fold in. Then fold in the crushed pineapple and the coconut.

3. Spoon the batter into the prepared pan and bake in the preheated oven for 25 minutes, or until a toothpick inserted into the center comes out clean.

4. Let cool in the pan for 10 minutes before turning out onto a wire rack to cool completely. To make the frosting, mix together the cream cheese and confectioners' sugar and spread over the cooled cake.

SOMETHING DIFFERENT Add a splash of coconut-flavor liqueur to the frosting.

Angel Food Cake

 SERVES 10    PREP TIME: 30 minutes plus cooling   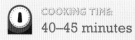 COOKING TIME: 40–45 minutes

nutritional information per serving	171 cal, 0.5g fat, 0.1g sat fat, 29g total sugars, 0.13g salt

This light fat-free sponge cake is topped with fresh berries and makes a great dessert for a summer barbecue or alfresco meal.

INGREDIENTS

sunflower oil, for greasing
8 extra-large egg whites
1 teaspoon cream of tartar
1 teaspoon almond extract
1¼ cups superfine sugar
1 cup all-purpose flour, plus extra for dusting

decoration

2 cups mixed berries, such as raspberries and blueberries
1 tablespoon lemon juice
2 tablespoons confectioners' sugar

1. Preheat the oven to 325°F. Grease and lightly flour a 9-inch tube pan.

2. In a clean, grease-free bowl, beat the egg whites until they hold soft peaks. Add the cream of tartar and beat again until the whites are stiff but not dry. Beat in the almond extract, then add the superfine sugar, a tablespoon at a time, beating hard between each addition. Sift in the flour and fold in lightly and evenly, using a large metal spoon.

3. Spoon the batter into the prepared cake pan. Bake in the preheated oven for 40–45 minutes, or until golden brown. Run the tip of a knife around the edges of the cake to loosen from the pan. Let cool in the pan for 10 minutes, then invert onto a wire rack to cool.

4. To decorate, place the berries, lemon juice, and confectioners' sugar in a saucepan and heat until the sugar has dissolved. Spoon over the top of the cake.

2

2

3

Chocolate Flake Cake

 SERVES 20    PREP TIME: 1 hour plus chilling    COOKING TIME: 2 hours

nutritional information per serving	650 cal, 38g fat, 23g sat fat, 56g total sugars, 0.5g salt

Making chocolate flakes, or curls, is a baking skill that's easy to achieve and adds a professional-looking touch to cakes.

INGREDIENTS

1 cup plus 3 tablespoons unsweetened cocoa powder

1¼ cups boiling water

9 ounces semisweet chocolate, melted

1¾ sticks salted butter, softened, plus extra for greasing

2¼ cups firmly packed light brown sugar

4 eggs, beaten

3 cups all-purpose flour

¾ teaspoon baking soda

4 teaspoons vanilla extract

ganache

18 ounces semisweet chocolate, chopped

2 cups heavy cream

¼ cup confectioners' sugar

decoration

7 ounces semisweet chocolate, chopped

⅓ cup brandy (optional)

rose petals or small edible flowers, to decorate (optional)

1. Preheat the oven to 325°F. Grease an 8-inch round cake pan and line with parchment paper. Beat the cocoa and water in a bowl until smooth, then stir in the chocolate. In another bowl, beat the butter and sugar until pale, then beat in the eggs, flour, baking soda, and vanilla. Stir in the chocolate mixture, then spoon into the prepared pan. Bake in the preheated oven for 2 hours, or until firm. Let cool.

2. For the decoration, place the chocolate in a heatproof bowl set over a saucepan of simmering water and heat until melted. Spread a thin layer on a cool slab. Let stand in a cool place until the chocolate is set but not brittle.

3. Push a wallpaper scraper or the edge of a metal spatula across the chocolate so that the chocolate starts to roll into loose curls. Place the flakes on a baking sheet lined with parchment paper and chill in the refrigerator while you finish the cake. Slice the cake in half horizontally. Drizzle the tops of the cake halves with brandy, if using.

4. To make the ganache, place the chocolate in a bowl. Heat the cream and confectioners' sugar in a saucepan and pour over the chocolate. Stir and let cool. Use one-quarter of the chocolate ganache to sandwich together the cake layers and place the cake on a flat serving plate or cake stand. Spread a thin layer of ganache around the sides of the cake with a spatula to seal in the crumbs. Chill in the refrigerator for 15 minutes. Spread the remaining ganache all over the cake in an even layer, smoothing it so it is flat or as textured as you desire. Sprinkle the flakes over the cake so the pieces fall at different angles. Sprinkle with rose petals or edible flowers, if using.

2

3

4

Cinnamon & Walnut Layer Cake

 SERVES 10    PREP TIME: 50 minutes plus cooling    COOKING TIME: 20–25 minutes

nutritional information per serving	788 cal, 55g fat, 21g sat fat, 51g total sugars, 0.6g salt

A moist and nutty layered cake with a creamy cinnamon-spiced frosting.

INGREDIENTS

1 cup firmly packed light brown sugar

2 cups all-purpose flour

2 teaspoons ground cinnamon, plus extra for dusting

1 teaspoon baking soda

3 eggs, beaten

1 cup sunflower oil, plus extra for greasing

1 cup finely chopped walnuts

1 large ripe banana, mashed

walnut pieces, to decorate

frosting

¾ cup cream cheese

2 sticks unsalted butter, softened

1 teaspoon ground cinnamon

1¾ cups confectioners' sugar, sifted

1. Preheat the oven to 350°F. Grease three 8-inch cake pans and line with parchment paper.

2. Put the brown sugar into a large bowl and sift in the flour, cinnamon, and baking soda. Add the eggs, oil, walnuts, and banana and beat with a wooden spoon until thoroughly mixed.

3. Divide the batter between the prepared pans and gently smooth the surfaces. Bake in the preheated oven for 20–25 minutes, or until golden brown and firm to the touch. Let cool in the pans for 10 minutes, then invert onto a wire rack to cool completely.

4. To make the frosting, put the cheese, butter, and cinnamon into a bowl and beat together until smooth and creamy. Stir in the confectioners' sugar and mix until smooth.

5. Sandwich together the three cakes with one-third of the frosting and spread the remainder over the top and sides of the cake. Decorate with the walnut pieces and a dusting of cinnamon.

2

4

5

Rich Fruitcake

 SERVES 16   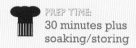 PREP TIME: 30 minutes plus soaking/storing   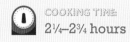 COOKING TIME: 2¼–2¾ hours

nutritional information per serving	400 cal, 16g fat, 8.5g sat fat, 49g total sugars, 0.15g salt

The cake of choice for a traditional Christmas celebration, this classic favorite should be made well in advance to allow time for the rich flavors to mature.

INGREDIENTS

2⅓ cups golden raisins

1½ cups raisins

¾ cup chopped dried apricots

⅔ cup chopped pitted dates

¼ cup dark rum or brandy, plus extra for flavoring (optional)

finely grated rind and juice of 1 orange

2 sticks unsalted butter, softened, plus extra for greasing

1 cup firmly packed light brown sugar

4 eggs, beaten

⅓ cup chopped candied peel

⅓ cup quartered candied cherries

2 pieces chopped candied ginger or preserved ginger

¼ cup blanched almonds, chopped

1⅔ cups all-purpose flour

1 teaspoon ground allspice

1. Place the golden raisins, raisins, apricots, and dates in a large bowl and stir in the rum, if using, orange rind, and orange juice. Cover and let soak for several hours or overnight.

2. Preheat the oven to 300°F. Grease an 8-inch round cake pan and line with parchment paper.

3. Beat together the butter and sugar in a large mixing bowl until pale and creamy. Gradually beat in the eggs, beating hard after each addition. Stir in the soaked fruits, candied peel, candied cherries, candied ginger, and blanched almonds.

4. Sift the flour and allspice over the beaten mixture, then fold in lightly and evenly. Spoon the batter into the prepared cake pan and smooth the surface, making a slight depression in the center with the back of the spoon.

5. Bake in the preheated oven for 2¼–2¾ hours, or until the cake begins to shrink away from the sides and a toothpick inserted into the center comes out clean. Cool completely in the pan.

6. Invert the cake and remove the parchment paper. Wrap in some wax paper and aluminum foil, and store for at least two months before use. To add a richer flavor, prick the cake with a toothpick and spoon over a couple of extra tablespoons of rum or brandy, if using, before storing.

1

4

4

Grasshopper Cake

 SERVES 12    PREP TIME: 50 minutes plus cooling    COOKING TIME: 1¼ hours

nutritional information per serving	667 cal, 39g fat, 24g sat fat, 59g total sugars, 0.8g salt

This decadent cake is made up of layers of rich moist chocolate cake with a creamy mint-flavored buttercream and decorated with grated chocolate.

INGREDIENTS

1 cup whole milk

1 tablespoon lemon juice

2¼ cups all-purpose flour

2 tablespoons unsweetened cocoa powder

1 teaspoon baking soda

1 tablespoon baking powder

1 stick salted butter, softened, plus extra for greasing

1 cup superfine sugar

2 extra-large eggs, beaten

4 ounces semisweet chocolate, melted

2 ounces milk chocolate, grated, to decorate

frosting

1¾ sticks unsalted butter, softened

1 cup heavy cream

3¼ cups confectioners' sugar

1 teaspoon peppermint extract

few drops of green food coloring

1. Preheat the oven to 325°F. Grease an 8-inch round cake pan and line with parchment paper.

2. Pour the milk into a bowl and add the lemon juice. Let stand for 15 minutes—the milk will start to curdle but this is ok.

3. Sift the flour, cocoa powder, baking soda, and baking powder into a large bowl. Add the butter, superfine sugar, and eggs and pour in the milk mixture. Beat with an electric handheld mixer until thoroughly combined. Beat in the melted chocolate.

4. Spoon the batter into the prepared pan and smooth the surface. Bake in the preheated oven for about 1¼ hours, or until the cake is risen and a toothpick inserted into the center comes out clean. Cool in the pan for 20 minutes, then invert onto a wire rack to cool completely.

5. For the frosting, place the butter in a bowl and beat with an electric handheld mixer for 2–3 minutes, or until pale and creamy. Beat in two-thirds of the cream, then gradually beat in the confectioners' sugar. Add the rest of the cream and continue beating for 1–2 minutes, or until the buttercream is light and fluffy. Stir in the peppermint extract and enough food coloring to produce a pale green color.

6. Slice the cake horizontally into three equal circles. Sandwich together the circles with half the buttercream frosting. Spread the remaining buttercream over the top and sides of the cake. Decorate with the chocolate shavings.

2

3

6

Maple & Pecan Bundt Cake

 SERVES 10

 PREP TIME:
30 minutes
plus cooling

 COOKING TIME:
45–50 minutes

nutritional information **per serving** | 466 cal, 28g fat, 14g sat fat, 33g total sugars, 0.6g salt

Baked in a classic fluted tube pan, this cake looks and tastes amazing.

INGREDIENTS

1¾ sticks salted butter, softened, plus extra for greasing

1 cup firmly packed light brown sugar

3 extra-large eggs, beaten

½ cup finely chopped pecans

¼ cup maple syrup

⅔ cup sour cream

1¾ cups all-purpose flour, plus extra for dusting

2¾ teaspoons baking powder

chopped pecan nuts, to decorate

icing

⅔ cup confectioners' sugar, sifted

1 tablespoon maple syrup

1–2 tablespoons lukewarm water

1. Preheat the oven to 325°F. Grease and lightly flour a 2-quart Bundt pan.

2. Put the butter and brown sugar into a bowl and beat together until pale and fluffy. Gradually beat in the eggs, then stir in the nuts, maple syrup, and sour cream. Sift in the flour and baking powder and fold in thoroughly.

3. Spoon the batter into the prepared pan and gently smooth the surface. Bake in the preheated oven for 45–50 minutes, or until the cake is firm and golden and a toothpick inserted into the center comes out clean. Let cool in the pan for 10 minutes, then invert onto a wire rack to cool completely.

4. To make the icing, mix the confectioners' sugar, maple syrup, and enough water to make a smooth icing. Spoon the icing over the top of the cake, letting it run down the sides. Decorate with the chopped nuts and let set.

2

3

3

Coffee & Walnut Cake

 SERVES 8

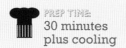 PREP TIME: 30 minutes plus cooling

 COOKING TIME: 20–25 minutes

nutritional information per serving	667 cal, 44g fat, 22g sat fat, 46g total sugars, 0.5g salt

Coffee and walnuts complement each other perfectly in this much-loved layer cake.

INGREDIENTS

1½ sticks unsalted butter, softened, plus extra for greasing
¾ cup firmly packed light bown sugar
3 extra-large eggs, beaten
3 tablespoons strong black coffee
1⅓ cups all-purpose flour
3½ teaspoons baking powder
1 cup walnut pieces
walnut halves, to decorate

frosting
1 stick unsalted butter, softened
1⅔ cups confectioners' sugar
1 tablespoon strong black coffee
½ teaspoon vanilla extract

1. Preheat the oven to 350°F. Grease two 8-inch cake pans and line with parchment paper.

2. Beat together the butter and brown sugar until pale and creamy. Gradually add the eggs, beating well after each addition. Beat in the coffee.

3. Sift the flour and baking powder into the mixture, then fold in lightly and evenly with a metal spoon. Fold in the walnut pieces. Divide the batter between the prepared cake pans and smooth the surfaces. Bake in the preheated oven for 20–25 minutes, or until golden brown and springy to the touch. Invert onto a wire rack to cool completely.

4. To make the frosting, beat together the butter, confectioners' sugar, coffee, and vanilla extract, mixing until smooth and creamy.

5. Use about half the mixture to sandwich the cakes together, then spread the remaining frosting on top and swirl with a spatula. Decorate with walnut halves.

2

3

5

COOK'S NOTE
For the best flavor, use a strong espresso coffee.

Classic Vanilla Cupcakes *68*

Red Velvet Cupcakes *70*

Devil's Food Chocolate Cupcakes *72*

Frosted Berry Cupcakes *74*

Ultimate Chocolate Cupcakes *76*

Pineapple Cupcakes *78*

Hummingbird Cupcakes *80*

Cherry Sundae Cupcakes *82*

White Chocolate & Rose Cupcakes *84*

Apple Streusel Cupcakes *86*

Tiramisu Cupcakes *88*

Candy Cupcakes *90*

Blueberry Muffins *92*

Chocolate Chip Muffins *94*

Raisin Bran Muffins *96*

Chocolate & Orange Muffins *98*

White Chocolate & Raspberry Muffins *100*

Peach Melba Muffins *102*

Chocolate & Sour Cherry Muffins *104*

Berry Muffins *106*

Irish Coffee Muffins *108*

Cranberry Muffins *110*

Fudge Nut Muffins *112*

Apple & Cinnamon Muffins *114*

Cupcakes & Muffins

Classic Vanilla Cupcakes

 MAKES 12    PREP TIME: 25 minutes   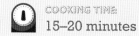 COOKING TIME: 15–20 minutes

nutritional information per cupcake	453 cal, 27g fat, 17g sat fat, 40g total sugars, 0.2g salt

Everyone's favorite—light and fluffy vanilla sponges topped with generous swirls of buttercream.

INGREDIENTS

1½ sticks unsalted butter, softened

1 cup superfine sugar

3 extra-large eggs, beaten

1 teaspoon vanilla extract

1⅓ cups all-purpose flour

2 teaspoons baking powder

frosting

1¼ sticks unsalted butter, softened

3 tablespoons heavy cream or whole milk

1 teaspoon vanilla extract

2⅓ cups confectioners' sugar, sifted

sprinkles, to decorate

1. Preheat the oven to 350°F. Place 12 muffin cups in a muffin pan.

2. Put the butter and superfine sugar into a bowl and beat together until pale and creamy. Gradually beat in the eggs and vanilla extract. Sift in the flour and baking powder and fold in gently.

3. Divide the batter evenly among the muffin cups and bake in the preheated oven for 15–20 minutes, or until risen and firm to the touch. Transfer to a wire rack and let cool.

4. To make the frosting, put the butter into a bowl and beat with an electric mixer for 2–3 minutes, or until pale and creamy. Beat in the cream and vanilla extract. Gradually beat in the confectioners' sugar and continue beating until the buttercream is light and fluffy.

5. Use a spatula to swirl the frosting over the tops of the cupcakes. Decorate with sprinkles.

SOMETHING DIFFERENT

To make bite-size cupcakes for children's parties, divide the batter among 30 mini cupcake liners and reduce the cooking time to 8-10 minutes.

Red Velvet Cupcakes

 MAKES 12

 PREP TIME:
25 minutes

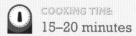 COOKING TIME:
15–20 minutes

nutritional information per cupcake	373 cal, 21g fat, 13g sat fat, 35.5g total sugars, 0.6g salt

Cocoa powder, buttermilk, and red food coloring give these favorites their deep rich color and wonderful flavor.

INGREDIENTS

1 cup all-purpose flour
1 teaspoon baking soda
2 tablespoons unsweetened cocoa powder
1 stick salted butter, softened
¾ cup superfine sugar
1 extra-large egg, beaten
½ cup buttermilk
1 teaspoon vanilla extract
1 tablespoon red food coloring
red colored sugar or red sugar sprinkles, to decorate

frosting
⅔ cup cream cheese
6 tablespoons unsalted butter, softened
2¼ cups confectioners' sugar, sifted

1. Preheat the oven to 350°F. Place 12 muffin cups in a muffin pan.

2. Sift together the flour, baking soda, and cocoa powder. Place the butter and superfine sugar in a bowl and beat together until pale and creamy. Gradually beat in the egg and half the flour mixture. Beat in the buttermilk, vanilla extract, and food coloring. Fold in the remaining flour mixture. Divide the batter evenly among the muffin cups.

3. Bake the cupcakes in the preheated oven for 15–20 minutes, or until risen and firm to the touch. Transfer to a wire rack and let cool.

4. To make the frosting, put the cream cheese and butter in a bowl and blend together with a spatula. Beat in the confectioners' sugar until smooth and creamy. Swirl the frosting on the top of the cupcakes. Sprinkle with the red sugar.

2

3

4

COOK'S NOTE
To color sugar red, place granulated sugar and 2-3 drops of red food coloring in a bag and mix together.

Devil's Food Chocolate Cupcakes

 MAKES 18  PREP TIME: 25 minutes plus chilling  COOKING TIME: 20 minutes

nutritional information
per cupcake | 155 cal, 8.5g fat, 4g sat fat, 13g total sugars, 0.2g salt

Based on the classic cake with the same name, these cupcakes will certainly please chocolate lovers!

INGREDIENTS

3½ tablespoons soft margarine
½ cup firmly packed dark brown sugar
2 extra-large eggs, beaten
1 cup all-purpose flour
½ teaspoon baking soda
¼ cup unsweetened cocoa powder
½ cup sour cream
chocolate flakes (see page 54)

frosting
4 ounces semisweet chocolate, broken into pieces
2 tablespoons superfine sugar
⅔ cup sour cream

1. Preheat the oven to 350°F. Place 18 muffin cups in a muffin pan.

2. Put the margarine, brown sugar, eggs, flour, baking soda, and cocoa powder in a large bowl and beat together until just smooth. Using a metal spoon, fold in the sour cream. Divide the batter evenly among the muffin cups.

3. Bake the cupcakes in the preheated oven for 20 minutes, or until well risen and firm to the touch. Transfer to a wire rack to cool.

4. To make the frosting, put the chocolate into a heatproof bowl set over a saucepan of gently simmering water and heat until melted, stirring occasionally. Remove from the heat and let cool slightly, then beat in the superfine sugar and sour cream until combined. Spread the frosting over the tops of the cupcakes and let set in the refrigerator. Serve decorated with chocolate flakes.

2

2
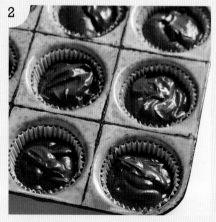

4

Frosted Berry Cupcakes

 MAKES 12   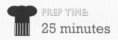 PREP TIME: 25 minutes   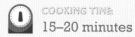 COOKING TIME: 15–20 minutes

nutritional information
per cupcake | 330 cal, 22.5g fat, 12.5g sat fat, 21g total sugars, 0.3g salt

These summer cupcakes are scented with orange flower water and topped with a creamy mascarpone frosting.

INGREDIENTS

1 stick salted butter, softened,
or ½ cup soft margarine
½ cup superfine sugar
2 teaspoons orange flower water
2 extra-large eggs, beaten
½ cup almond meal
(ground almonds)
1 cup all-purpose flour
1½ teaspoons baking powder
2 tablespoons milk
2½ cups mixed berries, fresh
mint leaves, egg white, and
sugar, to decorate

frosting

1¼ cups mascarpone cheese
⅓ cup superfine sugar
¼ cup orange juice

1. Preheat the oven to 350°F. Place 12 muffin cups in a muffin pan.

2. Place the butter, superfine sugar, and orange flower water in a large bowl and beat together until light and fluffy. Gradually beat in the eggs. Stir in the almond meal. Sift in the flour and baking powder and, using a metal spoon, fold in gently with the milk.

3. Divide the batter evenly among the muffin cups. Bake in the preheated oven for 15–20 minutes, or until risen, golden and firm to the touch. Transfer to a wire rack and let cool.

4. To make the frosting, put the mascarpone, superfine sugar, and orange juice in a bowl and beat together until smooth.

5. Swirl the frosting over the top of the cupcakes. Brush the berries and mint leaves with egg white, then roll in the sugar to coat. Decorate the cupcakes with the frosted berries and leaves.

2

5

5

COOK'S NOTE
Choose small berries,
such as blueberries
and raspberries, or
hull and halve or
quarter strawberries.

Ultimate Chocolate Cupcakes

 MAKES 14

 PREP TIME:
25 minutes
plus chilling

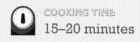 COOKING TIME:
15–20 minutes

nutritional information per cupcake	440 cal, 28g fat, 17g sat fat, 37g total sugars, 0.33g salt

Moist chocolate sponges topped with large swirls of rich and creamy frosting—these cupcakes are simply the best! Ideal for a special celebration or birthday because they can be made a day in advance.

INGREDIENTS

1 cup all-purpose flour
2 teaspoons baking powder
1½ tablespoons unsweetened cocoa powder
1 stick salted butter, softened, or ½ cup soft margarine
½ cup superfine sugar
2 extra-large eggs, beaten
2 ounces semisweet chocolate, melted

frosting
6 ounces semisweet chocolate, finely chopped
1 cup heavy cream
1¼ sticks unsalted butter, softened
2¼ cups confectioners' sugar, sifted
chocolate shapes and gold candied balls, to decorate (optional)

1. Preheat the oven to 350°F. Place 14 muffin cups in two muffin pans.

2. Sift the flour, baking powder, and cocoa powder into a large bowl. Add the butter, superfine sugar, and eggs and beat together until smooth. Fold in the melted chocolate.

3. Divide the batter evenly among the muffin cups. Bake in the preheated oven for 15–20 minutes, or until risen and firm to the touch. Transfer to a wire rack and let cool.

4. To make the frosting, put the chocolate in a heatproof bowl. Heat the cream in a saucepan until boiling, then pour over the chocolate and stir until smooth. Let cool, stirring occasionally, for 20 minutes, until thickened. Put the butter in a bowl, stir in the confectioners' sugar, and beat until smooth. Beat in the chocolate mixture. Chill for 15–20 minutes.

5. Spoon the frosting into a pastry bag fitted with a large star tip. Pipe swirls of frosting on top of each cupcake. Decorate with chocolate shapes and gold candied balls, if using.

2

2

4

Pineapple Cupcakes

 MAKES 12    PREP TIME: 25 minutes    COOKING TIME: 15–20 minutes

nutritional information per cupcake	400 cal, 24g fat, 16g sat fat, 36g total sugars, 0.2g salt

Pineapple and coconut are the perfect partners in these tropical-flavored cupcakes.

INGREDIENTS

1 stick unsalted butter, softened
½ cup superfine sugar
2 eggs, beaten
1 cup all-purpose flour
1½ teaspoons baking powder
3 canned pineapple slices, drained and finely chopped

frosting

1 stick unsalted butter, softened
½ cup cream cheese
2¼ cups confectioners' sugar, sifted
¾ cup dry unsweetened coconut
2 tablespoons chopped candied pineapple, to decorate

1. Preheat the oven to 350°F. Place 12 muffin cups in a muffin pan.

2. Put the butter and superfine sugar into a bowl and beat together until pale and creamy. Gradually beat in the eggs. Sift in the flour and baking powder and fold in gently. Fold in the chopped pineapple.

3. Divide the batter evenly among the muffin cups and bake in the preheated oven for 15–20 minutes, or until risen and firm to the touch. Transfer to a wire rack and let cool.

4. To make the frosting, beat together the butter and cream cheese until smooth. Gradually beat in the confectioners' sugar, then fold in the coconut.

5. Swirl the frosting over the tops of the cupcakes and decorate with the chopped candied pineapple.

3

3

4

Hummingbird Cupcakes

 MAKES 12    PREP TIME: 25 minutes    COOKING TIME: 15–20 minutes

nutritional information per cupcake	150 cal, 20g fat, 8g sat fat, 36g total sugars, 0.4g salt

These delicious cupcakes are packed with pineapple, banana, and pecans and lightly spiced with cinnamon. Decorated with a rich and creamy cream cheese frosting, they are as sweet as nectar!

INGREDIENTS

1¼ cups all-purpose flour
¾ teaspoon baking soda
1 teaspoon ground cinnamon
½ cup firmly packed light brown sugar
2 eggs, beaten
½ cup sunflower oil
1 ripe banana, mashed
2 canned pineapple slices, drained and finely chopped
¼ cup finely chopped pecans, plus extra sliced pecans to decorate

frosting
⅔ cup cream cheese
5 tablespoons unsalted butter, softened
1 teaspoon vanilla extract
2¼ cups confectioners' sugar, sifted

1. Preheat the oven to 350°F. Place 12 muffin cups in a muffin pan.

2. Sift the flour, baking soda, and cinnamon into a bowl and stir in the sugar. Add the eggs, oil, banana, pineapple, and chopped pecans and mix thoroughly. Divide the batter evenly among the muffin cups.

3. Bake the cupcakes in the preheated oven for 15–20 minutes, or until risen, golden, and firm to the touch. Transfer to a wire rack and let cool.

4. To make the frosting, put the cream cheese, butter, and vanilla extract in a bowl and blend together with a spatula. Beat in the confectioners' sugar until smooth and creamy. Pipe or swirl the frosting on the top of the cupcakes. Decorate with sliced pecans.

Cherry Sundae Cupcakes

 MAKES 12

 PREP TIME:
25 minutes
plus cooling

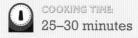 COOKING TIME:
25–30 minutes

nutritional information
per cupcake | 580 cal, 46g fat, 27g sat fat, 24g total sugars, 0.5g salt

Turn simple cherry and vanilla sponge cupcakes into something extra special by topping with big swirls of whipped cream, chocolate sauce, chopped nuts, and sugar sprinkles—children will love them!

INGREDIENTS

1½ sticks salted butter, softened,
or soft margarine
1 cup superfine sugar
3 eggs, beaten
1 teaspoon vanilla extract
1⅔ cups all-purpose flour
1½ teaspoons baking powder
¼ cup chopped candied cherries

chocolate sauce
3 ounces semisweet chocolate,
broken into pieces
2 tablespoons unsalted butter
1 tablespoon corn syrup

decoration
2½ cups heavy cream
2 tablespoons toasted,
chopped mixed nuts
pink cake-decorating glitter
12 maraschino cherries

1. Preheat the oven to 325°F. Place 12 muffin cups in a muffin pan.

2. Place the butter and superfine sugar in a large bowl and beat together until light and fluffy. Gradually beat in the eggs and vanilla extract. Sift in the flour and baking powder and, using a metal spoon, fold in gently. Fold in the candied cherries.

3. Divide the batter evenly among the muffin cups. Bake in the preheated oven for 25–30 minutes, or until risen, golden, and firm to the touch. Transfer to a wire rack and let cool.

4. To make the chocolate sauce, place the chocolate, butter, and syrup in a heatproof bowl set over a saucepan of simmering water and heat until melted. Remove from the heat and stir until smooth. Let cool, stirring occasionally, for 20–30 minutes.

5. Whip the cream until holding firm peaks. Spoon into a pastry bag fitted with a large star tip and pipe large swirls of cream on top of each cupcake. Drizzle with the chocolate sauce and sprinkle with the chopped nuts and pink glitter. Top each with a maraschino cherry.

4

5

5

White Chocolate & Rose Cupcakes

 MAKES 12

 PREP TIME:
25 minutes
plus chilling

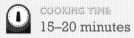 COOKING TIME:
15–20 minutes

nutritional information
per cupcake | 306 cal, 21g fat, 12.5g sat fat, 20g total sugars, 0.3g salt

These pretty cupcakes are delicately flavored with rose water and smothered in a creamy white chocolate frosting.

INGREDIENTS

1 stick unsalted butter, softened
½ cup superfine sugar
1 teaspoon rose water
2 eggs, beaten
1 cup all-purpose flour
1½ teaspoons baking powder
2 ounces white chocolate, grated
sugar frosted pink rose petals, to decorate

frosting
4 ounces white chocolate, broken into pieces
2 tablespoons whole milk
¾ cup cream cheese
¼ cup confectioners' sugar, sifted

1. Preheat the oven to 350°F. Place 12 muffin cups in a muffin pan.

2. Place the butter, sugar, and rose water in a bowl and beat together until pale and creamy. Gradually beat in the eggs. Sift the flour and baking powder over the mixture and fold in gently. Fold in the white chocolate. Divide the batter evenly among the muffin cups.

3. Bake the cupcakes in the preheated oven for 15–20 minutes, or until risen, golden, and firm to the touch. Transfer the cupcakes to a wire rack and let cool.

4. To make the frosting, place the chocolate and milk in a heatproof bowl set over a saucepan of simmering water and heat until melted. Remove from the heat and stir until smooth. Cool for 30 minutes. Put the cream cheese and confectioners' sugar in a bowl and beat together until smooth and creamy. Fold in the chocolate. Chill in the refrigerator for 1 hour. Swirl the frosting over the top of the cupcakes. Decorate with the sugar frosted rose petals.

2

3

4

SOMETHING DIFFERENT
Omit the rose water and replace with a teaspoon of dried and crushed lavender flowers. Decorate with fresh lavender sprigs.

Apple Streusel Cupcakes

 MAKES 14

 PREP TIME:
25 minutes

 COOKING TIME:
20 minutes

nutritional information
per cupcake | 160 cal, 6g fat, 3.5g sat fat, 13g total sugars, 0.3g salt

Topped with a spiced crumb, these fruity cupcakes make a great dessert served warm with whipped cream.

INGREDIENTS

½ teaspoon baking soda
1 cup applesauce (from a jar)
½ stick salted butter, softened
½ cup raw sugar
1 extra-large egg, beaten
1⅓ cups all-purpose flour
2 teaspoons baking powder
½ teaspoon ground cinnamon
½ teaspoon freshly grated nutmeg

topping
⅓ cup all-purpose flour
¼ cup raw sugar
¼ teaspoon ground cinnamon
¼ teaspoon freshly grated nutmeg
2½ tablespoons unsalted butter, softened

1. Preheat the oven to 350°F. Place 14 muffin cups in two muffin pans.

2. To make the topping, put the flour, raw sugar, cinnamon, and nutmeg in a bowl. Cut the butter into small pieces, then add to the bowl and rub it in with your fingertips until the mixture resembles fine bread crumbs.

3. Add the baking soda to the applesauce and stir until dissolved. Place the butter and raw sugar in a large bowl and beat together until pale and creamy. Gradually beat in the egg. Sift in the flour, baking powder, cinnamon, and nutmeg and, using a metal spoon, fold into the mixture, alternating with the applesauce mixture.

4. Divide the batter evenly among the muffin cups. Sprinkle the topping over the cupcakes and press down gently. Bake in the preheated oven for 20 minutes, or until risen, golden, and firm to the touch. Transfer to a wire rack and let cool.

2

3

3

FREEZING TIP
Freeze for up to two
months packed into a
freezer-proof container.
Let thaw at room
temperature for
2-3 hours.

Tiramisu Cupcakes

 MAKES 12    PREP TIME: 25 minutes plus cooling   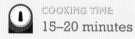 COOKING TIME: 15–20 minutes

nutritional information per cupcake	284 cal, 18g fat, 11g sat fat, 21g total sugars, 0.2g salt

These scrumptious cupcakes are like the classic Italian dessert—coffee, creamy mascarpone, and Marsala wine.

INGREDIENTS

1 stick unsalted butter, softened

½ cup firmly packed light brown sugar

2 eggs, beaten

1 cup all-purpose flour, sifted

2 teaspoons baking powder

2 teaspoons coffee granules

3 tablespoons confectioners' sugar

¼ cup water

2 tablespoons grated semisweet chocolate, for dusting

frosting

1 cup mascarpone cheese

⅓ cup superfine sugar

2 tablespoons Marsala wine or sweet sherry

1. Preheat the oven to 350°F. Place 12 muffin cups in a muffin pan.

2. Place the butter, brown sugar, eggs, flour, and baking powder in a bowl and beat together until pale and creamy. Divide the batter evenly among the muffin cups.

3. Bake the cupcakes in the preheated oven for 15–20 minutes, or until risen, golden, and firm to the touch.

4. Place the coffee granules, confectioners' sugar, and water in a saucepan and heat gently, stirring, until the coffee and sugar have dissolved. Boil for 1 minute, then let cool for 10 minutes. Brush the coffee syrup over the top of the warm cupcakes. Transfer the cupcakes to a wire rack and let cool.

5. For the frosting, put the mascarpone, sugar, and Marsala in a bowl and beat together until smooth. Spread over the top of the cakes. Using a star template, sprinkle the grated chocolate over the frosting.

2

4

5

BE PREPARED
The flavor of the cupcakes will improve if they are made a day in advance. Decorate just before serving.

Candy Cupcakes

 MAKES 12  PREP TIME: 25 minutes plus cooling  COOKING TIME: 18–22 minutes

nutritional information per cupcake	435 cal, 24g fat, 15g sat fat, 42g total sugars, 0.4g salt

These fun cupcakes will make a great treat for children's birthday parties. Why not let them try decorating the cakes themselves? Just make sure you have plenty of candies!

INGREDIENTS

1¼ sticks salted butter, softened, or ⅔ cup soft margarine
¾ cup superfine sugar
3 eggs, beaten
1¾ cups all-purpose flour
1¼ teaspoons baking powder
4 teaspoons strawberry-flavored popping candy
candies of your choice, to decorate (optional)

buttercream
1½ sticks unsalted butter, softened
2 tablespoons whole milk
2¾ cups confectioners' sugar
pink and yellow food colorings

1. Preheat the oven to 350°F. Place 12 muffin cups in a muffin pan.

2. Place the butter and superfine sugar in a large bowl and beat together until pale and creamy. Gradually beat in the eggs. Sift in the flour and baking powder and, using a metal spoon, fold in gently. Fold in half of the popping candy.

3. Divide the batter evenly among the muffin cups. Bake in the preheated oven for 18–22 minutes, or until risen, golden, and firm to the touch. Transfer to a wire rack and let cool.

4. To make the buttercream, place the butter in a bowl and beat until pale and creamy. Beat in the milk, then gradually sift in the confectioners' sugar and continue beating for 2–3 minutes, or until the buttercream is light and fluffy. Divide the buttercream between two bowls and beat a little pink or yellow food coloring into each bowl.

5. Pipe or swirl the buttercream on top of the cupcakes and decorate with candies, if using. Sprinkle over the remaining popping candy just before serving.

3

5

5

Blueberry Muffins

 MAKES 12    PREP TIME: 20 minutes    COOKING TIME: 20 minutes

nutritional information per muffin	200 cal, 8g fat, 1.5g sat fat, 12g total sugars, 0.5g salt

Dotted with juicy blueberries and flavored with lemon and vanilla, these buttery muffins will be snapped up as soon as they come out of the oven.

INGREDIENTS

2¼ cups all-purpose flour

1 tablespoon baking powder

pinch of salt

½ cup firmly packed light brown sugar

1 cup frozen blueberries

2 eggs

1 cup whole milk

6 tablespoons salted butter, melted and cooled

1 teaspoon vanilla extract

finely grated rind of 1 lemon

1. Preheat the oven to 400°F. Place 12 muffin cups in a muffin pan. Sift together the flour, baking powder, and salt into a large bowl. Stir in the sugar and blueberries.

2. Lightly beat the eggs in a bowl, then beat in the milk, melted butter, vanilla extract, and lemon rind. Make a well in the center of the dry ingredients and pour in the liquid ingredients. Stir gently until just combined; do not overmix.

3. Divide the batter evenly among the muffin cups. Bake in the preheated oven for about 20 minutes, or until well risen, golden brown, and firm to the touch.

4. Let the muffins cool in the pan for 5 minutes, then serve warm or transfer to a wire rack and let cool.

1

2

3

Chocolate Chip Muffins

 MAKES 12

 PREP TIME: 20 minutes

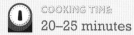 COOKING TIME: 20–25 minutes

nutritional information per muffin	252 cal, 11g fat, 6.5g sat fat, 15g total sugars, 0.6g salt

These classic muffins have a wonderful light texture and are full of delicious milk chocolate chunks.

INGREDIENTS

2⅓ cups all-purpose flour

5 teaspoons baking powder

6 tablespoons salted butter, chilled and diced

½ cup superfine sugar

6 ounces milk chocolate, chopped into chunks

2 extra-large eggs, beaten

1 cup buttermilk

1 teaspoon vanilla extract

1. Preheat the oven to 400°F. Place 12 muffin cups in a muffin pan.

2. Sift together the flour and baking powder into a large bowl. Add the butter and rub in to make fine bread crumbs. Stir in the sugar and the chocolate chunks.

3. Beat together the eggs, buttermilk, and vanilla extract. Make a well in the center of the dry ingredients and pour in the liquid ingredients. Stir gently until just combined; do not overmix.

4. Divide the batter evenly among the muffin cups. Bake in the preheated oven for 20–25 minutes, or until risen, golden, and just firm to the touch. Let cool for 5 minutes, then transfer to a wire rack to cool completely.

2

2

4

COOK'S NOTE
To make your own muffin cups, cut out 5-inch squares of parchment paper. Press them into the pan, smoothing down the folds.

Raisin Bran Muffins

 MAKES 12    PREP TIME: 20 minutes    COOKING TIME: 20 minutes

nutritional information
per muffin   211 cal, 8g fat, 1.5g sat fat, 19g total sugars, 0.47g salt

Great for a quick and filling breakfast on the go or mid afternoon snack, these high-fiber fruity muffins will keep hunger pangs at bay.

INGREDIENTS

1 cup plus 2 tablespoons all-purpose flour

1 tablespoon baking powder

2½ cups wheat bran

½ cup superfine sugar

1 cup raisins

2 eggs

1 cup skim milk

⅓ cup sunflower oil

1 teaspoon vanilla extract

1. Preheat the oven to 400°F. Place 12 muffin cups in a muffin pan. Sift together the flour and baking powder into a large bowl. Stir in the bran, sugar, and raisins.

2. Lightly beat the eggs in a bowl, then beat in the milk, oil, and vanilla extract. Make a well in the center of the dry ingredients and pour in the liquid ingredients. Stir gently until just combined; do not overmix.

3. Divide the batter evenly among the muffin cups. Bake in the preheated oven for about 20 minutes, or until well risen, golden brown, and firm to the touch.

4. Let the muffins cool in the pan for 5 minutes, then serve warm or transfer to a wire rack and let cool.

SOMETHING
DIFFERENT
Replace the
raisins with
chopped dried
apricots or
sweetened dried
cranberries.

Chocolate & Orange Muffins

 MAKES 12  PREP TIME: 20 minutes plus cooling  COOKING TIME: 20 minutes

nutritional information per muffin	408 cal, 21g fat, 9.5g sat fat, 37g total sugars, 0.8g salt

These sweet and crumbly muffins are full of chocolate chips and flavored with tangy orange zest and juice. To make them even more delicious, they have a rich chocolate buttercream topping.

INGREDIENTS

2 oranges

about ½ cup milk

1¾ cups all-purpose flour

⅔ cup unsweetened cocoa powder

1 tablespoon baking powder

pinch of salt

½ cup firmly packed light brown sugar

1 cup semisweet chocolate chips

2 eggs

⅓ cup sunflower oil or 6 tablespoons salted butter, melted and cooled

strips of orange zest, to decorate

frosting

2 ounces semisweet chocolate, broken into pieces

2 tablespoons unsalted butter

2 tablespoons water

1⅓ cups confectioners' sugar

1. Preheat the oven to 400°F. Place 12 muffin cups in a muffin pan.

2. Finely grate the rind from the oranges and squeeze the juice. Add enough milk to make up the juice to 1 cup, then add the orange rind. Sift together the flour, cocoa, baking powder, and salt into a large bowl. Stir in the brown sugar and chocolate chips. Place the eggs in a bowl and beat lightly, then beat in the milk-and-orange mixture and the oil. Make a well in the center of the dry ingredients and pour in the liquid ingredients. Stir gently until just combined; do not overmix. Divide the batter evenly among the muffin cups.

3. Bake in the preheated oven for 20 minutes, or until well risen and firm to the touch. Let cool in the pan for 5 minutes, then transfer to a wire rack to cool completely.

4. To make the frosting, place the chocolate in a heatproof bowl, add the butter and water, then set the bowl over a saucepan of gently simmering water and heat, stirring, until melted. Remove from the heat and sift in the confectioners' sugar. Beat until smooth, then spread the frosting on top of the muffins and decorate with strips of orange zest.

White Chocolate & Raspberry Muffins

 MAKES 12    PREP TIME: 20 minutes    COOKING TIME: 20–25 minutes

nutritional information per muffin	246 cal, 11g fat, 6.5g sat fat, 18g total sugars, 0.5g salt

Best eaten warm from the oven, these muffins make a great mid morning snack.

INGREDIENTS

2 cups all-purpose flour

1 tablespoon baking powder

½ cup superfine sugar

6 tablespoons salted butter, chilled and coarsely grated

1 extra-large egg, beaten

¾ cup whole milk

1½ cups raspberries

¾ cup white chocolate chips

1. Preheat the oven to 400°F. Place 12 muffin cups in a muffin pan.

2. Sift together the flour and baking powder into a large bowl and stir in the sugar. Add the butter and stir with a fork to coat in the flour mixture. Lightly beat the egg in a bowl, then beat in the milk.

3. Make a well in the center of the dry ingredients and pour in the liquid ingredients. Stir gently until just combined; do not overmix. Fold in the raspberries and half of the chocolate chips.

4. Divide the batter evenly among the muffin cups and sprinkle the remaining chocolate chips over the muffins. Bake in the preheated oven for 20–25 minutes, or until risen, golden, and just firm to the touch. Let cool for 5 minutes, then transfer to a wire rack to cool completely.

SOMETHING
DIFFERENT
Replace the
raspberries with
fresh or frozen
blackberries,
or try chopped
fresh mango for
a tropical flavor.

Peach Melba Muffins

 MAKES 12    PREP TIME: 20 minutes    COOKING TIME: 20–25 minutes

nutritional information per muffin	228 cal, 10g fat, 6g sat fat, 14g total sugars, 0.6g salt

Soft muffins packed with peaches and fresh raspberries and a crunchy nut and sugar topping—sensational!

INGREDIENTS

2¼ cups all-purpose flour

5 teaspoons baking powder

½ cup frimly packed light brown sugar

1 extra-large egg

⅔ cup whole milk

1 stick salted butter, melted and cooled

1 cup fresh raspberries

1 cup chopped, drained canned peach slices

1 tablespoon chopped mixed nuts

1 tablespoon demerara sugar or other raw sugar

1. Preheat the oven to 400°F. Place 12 muffin cups in a muffin pan. Sift together the flour and baking powder into a large bowl. Stir in the brown sugar.

2. Lightly beat the egg in a bowl, then beat in the milk and melted butter. Make a well in the center of the dry ingredients and pour in the liquid ingredients. Stir gently until just combined; do not overmix.

3. Gently fold in the raspberries and peaches. Divide the batter evenly among the muffin cups. Mix together the nuts and demerara sugar and sprinkle over the top of the muffins. Bake in the preheated oven for 20–25 minutes, or until well risen, golden, and firm to the touch.

4. Let the muffins cool in the pan for 5 minutes, then serve warm or transfer to a wire rack and let cool.

2

3

3

Chocolate & Sour Cherry Muffins

 MAKES 12

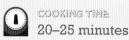 PREP TIME: 20 minutes plus cooling

 COOKING TIME: 20–25 minutes

nutritional information per muffin	244 cal, 12g fat, 7g sat fat, 16g total sugars, 0.7g salt

These luxury muffins are studded with dried sour cherries and topped with a glossy chocolate glaze.

INGREDIENTS

1¾ cups all-purpose flour

1 tablespoon baking powder

½ cup unsweetened cocoa powder

½ cup firmly packed light brown sugar

6 tablespoons salted butter, chilled and coarsely grated

2 eggs

¾ cup whole milk

⅓ cup dried sour cherries

1 tablespoon semisweet chocolate shavings

glaze

2 ounces semisweet chocolate, broken into pieces

2 tablespoons unsalted butter

1. Preheat the oven to 400°F. Place 12 muffin cups in a muffin pan. Sift together the flour, baking powder, and cocoa powder into a large bowl. Stir in the sugar. Add the grated butter and stir with a fork to coat in the flour mixture.

2. Lightly beat the eggs in a bowl, then beat in the milk. Make a well in the center of the dry ingredients and pour in the liquid ingredients. Stir gently until just combined; do not overmix. Gently fold in the dried cherries.

3. Divide the batter evenly among the muffin cups. Bake in the preheated oven for 20–25 minutes, or until well risen and firm to the touch. Let the muffins cool in the pan for 5 minutes, then transfer to a wire rack and let cool.

4. For the glaze, melt the chocolate with the butter in a heatproof bowl set over a saucepan of gently simmering water. Let cool for 15 minutes, then spoon over the tops of the muffins and sprinkle with the chocolate shavings.

1

2

4

COOK'S NOTE Use a vegetable peeler to make the chocolate shavings.

Berry Muffins

 MAKES 12    PREP TIME: 20 minutes   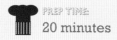 COOKING TIME: 20–25 minutes

nutritional information per muffin	255 cal, 15g fat, 7g sat fat, 13g total sugars, 0.5g salt

Quick and easy to make, these muffins are packed full of fresh mixed berries.

INGREDIENTS

1¾ cups all-purpose flour

2 teaspoons baking powder

½ cup almond meal (ground almonds)

⅔ cup superfine sugar, plus extra for sprinkling

1¼ sticks salted butter, melted

½ cup milk

2 eggs, beaten

2 cups mixed berries, such as blueberries, raspberries, and blackberries

1. Preheat the oven to 375°F. Place 12 muffin cups in a muffin pan.

2. Sift together the flour and baking powder into a large bowl and stir in the almond meal and sugar. Make a well in the center of the dry ingredients.

3. Beat together the butter, milk, and eggs and pour into the well. Stir gently until just combined; do not overmix. Gently fold in the berries.

4. Divide the batter evenly among the muffin cups. Bake in the preheated oven for 20–25 minutes, or until light golden and just firm to the touch. Serve warm or cold, sprinkled with sugar.

FREEZING TIP
The muffins will
freeze for up
to two months.
Thaw at room
temperature for
1-2 hours.

Irish Coffee Muffins

 MAKES 12    PREP TIME: 20 minutes    COOKING TIME: 20 minutes

nutritional information per muffin	232 cal, 13g fat, 8g sat fat, 6g total sugars, 0.6g salt

Whiskey, coffee liqueur, and heavy cream turn a basic muffin into an impressive sweet treat for a special occasion.

INGREDIENTS

2¼ cups all-purpose flour

1 tablespoon baking powder

pinch of salt

6 tablespoons salted butter

¼ cup firmly packed light brown sugar

1 extra-large egg, beaten

½ cup heavy cream

1 teaspoon almond extract

2 tablespoons strong coffee

2 tablespoons coffee-flavored liqueur

¼ cup Irish whiskey

whipped cream and unsweetened cocoa powder, to serve (optional)

1. Preheat the oven to 400°F. Place 12 muffin cups in a muffin pan. Sift together the flour, baking powder, and salt into a large bowl.

2. In a separate large bowl, cream together the butter and sugar, then stir in the egg. Mix in the heavy cream, almond extract, coffee, liqueur, and whiskey. Make a well in the center of the dry ingredients and pour in the liquid ingredients. Stir gently until just combined; do not overmix.

3. Divide the batter evenly among the muffin cups. Bake in the preheated oven for 20 minutes, or until well risen, golden brown, and firm to the touch.

4. Let the muffins cool in the pan for 5 minutes, then transfer to a wire rack to cool completely. If desired, pipe a swirl of whipped cream over the top of each muffin and dust with cocoa powder. Chill the muffins in the refrigerator until ready to serve.

SOMETHING DIFFERENT
For bite-size muffins,
divide the batter among
30 mini cupcake
liners and bake for
10-12 minutes.

Cranberry Muffins

  MAKES 10   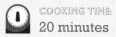 PREP TIME: 20 minutes   COOKING TIME: 20 minutes

nutritional information per muffin	170 cal, 7g fat, 1g sat fat, 7g total sugars, 0.4g salt

Cranberries, apples, and marmalade combine to make these tasty muffins that are not too sweet.

INGREDIENTS

1⅓ cups all-purpose white flour

½ cup whole-wheat flour

1 teaspoon ground cinnamon

½ teaspoon baking soda

2¾ teaspoons baking powder

1 egg

¼ cup fine-cut marmalade

⅔ cup skim milk or low-fat milk

⅓ cup sunflower oil, plus extra for greasing

1 small apple, such as Pippin, peeled, cored, and finely diced

1 cup fresh or frozen cranberries, thawed if frozen

1 tablespoon rolled oats

1. Preheat the oven to 400°F. Place 10 muffin cups in a muffin pan or grease a silicon muffin pan. Sift together the flours, cinnamon, baking soda, and baking powder into a large bowl, adding any husks that remain in the sifter or strainer.

2. Lightly beat the egg with the marmalade in a bowl, then beat in the milk and oil. Make a well in the center of the dry ingredients and pour in the liquid ingredients. Stir gently until just combined; do not overmix. Stir in the apple and cranberries.

3. Divide the batter evenly among the muffin cups and sprinkle the oats over the tops of the muffins. Bake in the preheated oven for about 20 minutes, or until well risen, golden brown, and firm to the touch.

4. Let the muffins cool in the pan for 5 minutes, then serve warm or transfer to a wire rack and let cool.

FREEZING TIP
Freeze for up
to two months
in freezer bags.
Thaw at room
temperature for
2-3 hours.

Fudge Nut Muffins

 MAKES 12    PREP TIME: 20 minutes   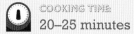 COOKING TIME: 20–25 minutes

nutritional information per muffin	280 cal, 13g fat, 5g sat fat, 18g total sugars, 0.6g salt

Peanut butter gives these muffins a wonderful nutty flavor and a beautiful crunchy texture.

INGREDIENTS

2 cups all-purpose flour

4 teaspoons baking powder

⅓ cup superfine sugar

⅓ cup chunky peanut butter

1 extra-large egg

¾ cup whole milk

4 tablespoons salted butter, melted and cooled

5½ ounces vanilla fudge, cut into small pieces

3 tablespoons coarsely chopped unsalted peanuts

1. Preheat the oven to 400°F. Place 12 muffin cups in a muffin pan. Sift together the flour and baking powder into a large bowl. Stir in the sugar. Add the peanut butter and stir until the mixture resembles bread crumbs.

2. Lightly beat the egg in a bowl, then beat in the milk and melted butter. Make a well in the center of the dry ingredients, pour in the liquid ingredients, and add the fudge pieces. Stir gently until just combined; do not overmix.

3. Divide the batter evenly among the muffin cups. Sprinkle the peanuts over the tops of the muffins. Bake in the preheated oven for 20–25 minutes, or until well risen, golden brown, and firm to the touch.

4. Let the muffins cool in the pan for 5 minutes, then serve warm or transfer to a wire rack and let cool.

COOK'S NOTE
To refresh day-old muffins, put in a preheated moderate oven for 5-10 minutes.

Apple & Cinnamon Muffins

 MAKES 12    PREP TIME: 20 minutes    COOKING TIME: 20–25 minutes

nutritional information per muffin	210 cal, 9g fat, 2g sat fat, 13g total sugars, 0.3g salt

Wholesome muffins made with oats, brown sugar, and grated apple—delicious warm from the oven.

INGREDIENTS

1⅔ cups whole-wheat all-purpose flour

¾ cup rolled oats

2 teaspoons baking powder

1 teaspoon ground cinnamon

½ cup firmly packed light brown sugar

2 extra-large eggs

1 cup low-fat milk

½ cup sunflower oil

1 teaspoon vanilla extract

1 large apple, such as Pippin, peeled, cored, and grated

1. Preheat the oven to 350°F. Place 12 muffin cups in a muffin pan.

2. Sift together the flour, oats, baking powder, and cinnamon into a large bowl, adding any husks that remain in the sifter or strainer. Stir in the sugar.

3. Lightly beat the eggs in a bowl, then beat in the milk, oil, and vanilla extract. Make a well in the center of the dry ingredients and pour in the liquid ingredients. Stir gently until just combined; do not overmix. Stir in the apple.

4. Divide the batter evenly among the muffin cups. Bake in the preheated oven for 20–25 minutes, or until well risen, golden brown, and firm to the touch.

5. Let the muffins cool in the pan for 5 minutes, then serve warm or transfer to a wire rack and let cool.

2

3

3

Double Chocolate Whoopie Pies *118*

Vanilla Whoopie Pies *120*

Snickerdoodle Whoopie Pies *122*

Mini Carrot Cakes *124*

Mini Strawberry Layer Cakes *126*

Blueberry Scones *128*

Cinnamon Scones *130*

Cranberry & Orange Scones *132*

Chocolate & Cinnamon Brownies *134*

Chocolate & Cherry Brownies *136*

Vanilla Fudge Blondies *138*

Double Chocolate Pecan Blondies *140*

Vanilla Cake Pops *142*

Chocolate Mint Rocky Road Pops *144*

Chewy Marshmallow Bars *146*

Rocky Road Bars *148*

Date, Pistachio & Honey Slices *150*

Vanilla Macaroons *152*

Salted Caramel Squares *154*

Chocolate Fudge *156*

Coconut & Raspberry Squares *158*

Apricot Oat Bars *160*

Ginger & Chocolate Oat Bars *162*

Raisin Oat Bars *164*

Small Cakes & Bars

Double Chocolate Whoopie Pies

 MAKES 12

 PREP TIME:
30 minutes
plus chilling

 COOKING TIME:
20–25 minutes

nutritional information per cake	480 cal, 35g fat, 19g sat fat, 26g total sugars, 0.8g salt

What could be more delicious than two little cakes sandwiched together with a creamy filling? This double chocolate version is simply irresistible.

INGREDIENTS

1⅔ cups all-purpose flour

1½ teaspoons baking soda

¼ cup unsweetened cocoa powder

large pinch of salt

6 tablespoons salted butter, softened

⅓ cup vegetable shortening

⅔ cup firmly packed, light brown sugar

1 ounce semisweet chocolate, finely grated

1 extra-large egg, beaten

½ cup whole milk

¼ cup semisweet chocolate strands

white chocolate filling

6 ounces white chocolate, broken into pieces

2 tablespoons milk

1¼ cups heavy cream

1. Preheat the oven to 350°F. Line two to three large baking sheets with parchment paper. Sift together the all-purpose flour, baking soda, cocoa powder, and salt.

2. Place the butter, vegetable shortening, sugar, and grated chocolate in a large bowl and beat with an electric handheld mixer until pale and fluffy. Beat in the egg, followed by half the flour mixture, then the milk. Stir in the rest of the flour mixture and mix until thoroughly incorporated.

3. Pipe or spoon 24 mounds of the batter onto the prepared baking sheets, spaced well apart to allow for spreading. Bake in the preheated oven, one sheet at a time, for 10–12 minutes, or until risen and just firm to the touch. Cool for 5 minutes, then, using a spatula, transfer to a wire rack and let cool completely.

4. For the filling, place the chocolate and milk in a heatproof bowl set over a saucepan of simmering water. Heat until the chocolate has melted, stirring occasionally. Remove from the heat and let cool for 30 minutes. Using an electric mixer, whip the cream until holding firm peaks. Fold in the chocolate. Cover and chill in the refrigerator for 30–45 minutes, or until firm enough to spread.

5. To assemble, spread or pipe the chocolate filling on the flat side of half of the cakes. Top with the rest of the cakes. Spread the chocolate strands on a plate and gently roll the edges of each whoopie pie in the strands to lightly coat.

Vanilla Whoopie Pies

 MAKES 12    PREP TIME: 30 minutes plus chilling    COOKING TIME: 20–25 minutes

nutritional information per cake	445 cal, 24g fat, 15g sat fat, 39g total sugars, 0.7g salt

These soft vanilla sponges are filled with a rich chocolate buttercream. Serve with a large mug of coffee for a delicious mid morning treat.

INGREDIENTS

2 cups all-purpose flour
1 teaspoon baking soda
large pinch of salt
1½ sticks salted butter, softened
¾ cup superfine sugar
1 extra-large egg, beaten
2 teaspoons vanilla extract
⅔ cup buttermilk

chocolate buttercream filling
4 ounces milk chocolate, broken into pieces
1 stick unsalted butter, softened
2 cups confectioners' sugar, sifted

1. Preheat the oven to 350°F. Line two to three large baking sheets with parchment paper. Sift together the all-purpose flour, baking soda, and salt.

2. Place the butter and sugar in a large bowl and beat with an electric handheld mixer until pale and fluffy. Beat in the egg and vanilla extract, followed by half the flour mixture, and then the buttermilk. Stir in the rest of the flour mixture and mix until thoroughly incorporated.

3. Pipe or spoon 24 mounds of the batter onto the prepared baking sheets, spaced well apart to allow for spreading. Bake in the preheated oven, one sheet at a time, for 10–12 minutes, or until risen and just firm to the touch. Cool for 5 minutes, then, using a spatula, transfer to a wire rack and let cool completely.

4. For the filling, place the chocolate in a heatproof bowl set over a saucepan of simmering water and heat until melted. Remove from the heat and let cool for 20 minutes, stirring occasionally. Place the butter in a bowl and beat with an electric mixer for 2–3 minutes, or until pale and creamy. Gradually beat in the confectioners' sugar, then beat in the chocolate.

5. To assemble, spread or pipe the buttercream on the flat side of half of the cakes. Top with the rest of the cakes.

Snickerdoodle Whoopie Pies

 MAKES 15

 PREP TIME:
30 minutes
plus chilling

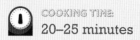 COOKING TIME:
20–25 minutes

nutritional information per cake	325 cal, 16g fat, 10g sat fat, 31g total sugars, 0.6g salt

Based on the classic cookie, these whoopie pies have a sweet sugary cinnamon coating and a creamy coffee filling. Wrapped individually, they will keep in the refrigerator for two to three days.

INGREDIENTS

2 cups all-purpose flour

1 teaspoon baking soda

large pinch of salt

2 teaspoons ground cinnamon

1 stick salted butter, softened

¾ cup superfine sugar, plus 2 tablespoons for sprinkling

1 extra-large egg, beaten

1 teaspoon vanilla extract

⅔ cup buttermilk

coffee filling

1 stick unsalted butter, softened

¾ cup cream cheese

1 tablespoon strong, cold black coffee

2¼ cups confectioners' sugar, sifted

1. Preheat the oven to 350°F. Line two to three large baking sheets with parchment paper. Sift together the flour, baking soda, salt, and 1 teaspoon of the cinnamon.

2. Place the butter and the ¾ cup of superfine sugar in a large bowl and beat with an electric handheld mixer until pale and fluffy. Beat in the egg and vanilla extract, followed by half the flour mixture, and then the buttermilk. Stir in the rest of the flour mixture and mix until thoroughly incorporated.

3. Pipe or spoon 30 mounds of the batter onto the prepared baking sheets, spaced well apart to allow for spreading. Mix together the rest of the cinnamon with the 2 tablespoons of superfine sugar and sprinkle liberally over the mounds. Bake in the preheated oven, one sheet at a time, for 10–12 minutes, or until risen and just firm to the touch. Cool for 5 minutes, then, using a spatula, transfer to a wire rack and let cool completely.

4. For the filling, place the butter, cream cheese, and coffee in a bowl and beat together until well blended. Gradually beat in the confectioners' sugar until smooth.

5. To assemble, spread or pipe the coffee filling on the flat side of half of the cakes. Top with the rest of the cakes.

1

4

5

Mini Carrot Cakes

 MAKES 20

 PREP TIME:
1 hour
plus cooling

 COOKING TIME:
35 minutes

nutritional information per cake	250 cal, 15.5g fat, 8g sat fat, 19g total sugars, 0.32g salt

Carrot cake is such an all-time favorite, it had to be included here. If you're making these in advance, the little marzipan carrots can be positioned after frosting the cake.

INGREDIENTS

1¼ sticks salted butter, softened, plus extra for greasing

¾ cup firmly packed light brown sugar

3 eggs, beaten

1¼ cups all-purpose flour

2 teaspoons baking powder

½ teaspoon ground allspice

1 cup almond meal (ground almonds)

finely grated rind of 1 lemon

1⅓ cups shredded carrots

½ cup coarsely chopped golden raisins

decoration

⅔ cup cream cheese

3 tablespoons unsalted butter, softened

1 cup confectioners' sugar, plus extra for dusting

2 tablespoons lemon juice

2¼ ounces marzipan

orange food coloring

several sprigs of dill

1. Preheat the oven to 350°F. Grease a 10-inch x 8-inch baking pan and line with parchment paper. Grease the parchment paper. Put the butter, light brown sugar, eggs, flour, baking powder, allspice, almond meal, and lemon rind in a mixing bowl and beat together with an electric handheld mixer until smooth and creamy. Stir in the carrots and golden raisins.

2. Spoon the batter into the prepared pan and smooth the surface. Bake in the preheated oven for 35 minutes, or until risen and just firm to the touch. Let cool in the pan for 10 minutes, then transfer to a wire rack to cool.

3. For the decoration, beat together the cream cheese, butter, confectioners' sugar, and lemon juice until creamy. Color the marzipan deep orange by dabbing a few drops of the food coloring onto the marzipan and rolling out the marzipan on a surface lightly dusted with confectioners' sugar until the color is evenly mixed. Roll the marzipan into a sausage shape, then divide it into 20 pieces and form each one into a small carrot shape, marking shallow grooves around each with a knife.

4. Using a spatula, spread the frosting over the cake, taking it almost to the edges. Trim the crusts from the cake to neaten it, then cut it into 20 squares. Place a marzipan carrot on each cake and add a small sprig of dill.

1

2

4

Mini Strawberry Layer Cakes

 MAKES 12  PREP TIME: 20 minutes plus cooling COOKING TIME: 15 minutes

nutritional information per cake	211 cal, 13g fat, 8g sat fat, 18g total sugars, 0.2g salt

So tiny and dainty, these cakes are just right with coffee when you don't want anything too rich or filling.

INGREDIENTS

5 tablespoons salted butter, softened, plus extra for greasing

⅓ cup superfine sugar

½ cup all-purpose flour

¾ teaspoon baking powder

1 egg, beaten

1 egg yolk

1 teaspoon vanilla extract

decoration

⅓ cup heavy cream

⅓ cup strawberry preserves

⅔ cup confectioners' sugar

1 tablespoon lemon juice

1. Preheat the oven to 350°F. Grease a small muffin pan or line with 12 cupcake liners. Put the butter, superfine sugar, flour, baking powder, egg, egg yolk, and vanilla in a mixing bowl and beat together with an electric handheld mixer until smooth and creamy.

2. Using a teaspoon, spoon the batter evenly into the prepared pan and level with the back of the spoon. Bake in the preheated oven for 15 minutes, or until risen and just firm to the touch. Let cool in the pan for 5 minutes, then transfer to a wire rack to cool. Slice the cakes in half, using a sharp knife.

3. For the decoration, whip the cream until it just peaks. Press 2 tablespoons of the preserves through a strainer into a bowl to extract the seeds. Put the strained jam in a pastry bag and snip off the tip. Sandwich together the cakes with the remaining preserves and cream. Beat the confectioners' sugar and lemon juice in a bowl until smooth. Spoon the icing over the cakes, spreading just to the edges. Pipe dabs of preserves on each cake and draw a toothpick through them to create swirls.

2

3

3

SOMETHING DIFFERENT Replace the strawberry preserves with apricot preserves.

Blueberry Scones

 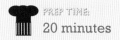 

MAKES 8

PREP TIME:
20 minutes

COOKING TIME:
20–22 minutes

nutritional information per cake	257 cal, 10g fat, 6g sat fat, 13g total sugars, 0.7g salt

These soft scone wedges are bursting with fresh blueberries and are delicious halved and lightly buttered warm from the oven.

INGREDIENTS

2 cups all-purpose flour, plus extra for dusting

2 teaspoons baking powder

¼ teaspoon salt

6 tablespoons salted butter, chilled and diced, plus extra for greasing and to serve

⅓ cup superfine sugar

1 cup blueberries

1 egg

½ cup buttermilk

1 tablespoon milk

1 tablespoon demerara sugar or other raw sugar

1. Preheat the oven to 400°F. Lightly grease a large baking sheet.

2. Sift together the flour, baking powder, and salt into a large bowl and stir in the butter. Rub the butter into the flour until the mixture resembles fine bread crumbs. Stir in the superfine sugar and blueberries.

3. Beat together the egg and buttermilk and pour into the bowl. Mix to a soft dough. Turn out the dough onto a floured surface and knead gently.

4. Shape and gently pat the dough into a 7-inch circle. Use a sharp knife to cut into eight even wedges. Place the wedges on the prepared baking sheet. Brush the tops of the scones with the milk and sprinkle with the demerara sugar. Bake in the preheated oven for 20–22 minutes, or until risen and golden brown. Transfer to a wire rack to cool and then serve with butter.

2

3

4

SOMETHING
DIFFERENT
You can use frozen
blueberries if fresh are
unavailable or replace
them with 1 cup dried
sweetened blueberries.

Cinnamon Scones

 MAKES 8   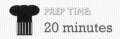 PREP TIME: 20 minutes   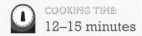 COOKING TIME: 12–15 minutes

nutritional information per cake	241 cal, 7g fat, 4.5g sat fat, 18g total sugars, 0.9g salt

These fruit biscuitlike scones are lightly spiced with cinnamon and drizzled with a sweet cinnamon icing.

INGREDIENTS

2 cups all-purpose flour, plus extra for dusting

4½ teaspoons baking powder

pinch of salt

1 teaspoon ground cinnamon

4 tablespoons salted butter, chilled and diced, plus extra for greasing and to serve

3 tablespoons superfine sugar

⅓ cup golden raisins

⅔ cup whole milk, plus extra for glazing

icing

½ cup confectioners' sugar

½ teaspoon ground cinnamon

1–2 tablespoons lukewarm water

1. Preheat the oven to 425°F. Lightly grease a large baking sheet and dust with flour.

2. Sift together the flour, baking powder, salt, and cinnamon into a large bowl and stir in the butter. Rub the butter in until the mixture resembles fine bread crumbs. Stir in the superfine sugar and raisins.

3. Pour in the milk and mix to a soft dough. Turn out onto a floured surface and knead lightly until smooth. Roll out to a thickness of ¾ inch. Using a 2¾-inch round cutter, stamp out eight circles, rerolling the dough as necessary.

4. Place the scones on the prepared baking sheet and glaze with milk. Bake in the preheated oven for 12–15 minutes, or until risen and golden. Transfer to a wire rack to cool.

5. To make the icing, sift together the confectioners' sugar and cinnamon into a bowl and stir in enough water to make a smooth icing. Drizzle the icing over the scones and let set. Serve with butter.

GOES WELL WITH

Make a tangy orange butter to spread on the halved scones by beating orange zest into softened unsalted butter.

Cranberry & Orange Scones

 MAKES 6  PREP TIME: 20 minutes  COOKING TIME: 20 minutes

nutritional information per cake | 375 cal, 14g fat, 8g sat fat, 12g total sugars, 0.9g salt

These tasty scones are a great thing to have for breakfast on Christmas Day.

INGREDIENTS

2½ cups all-purpose flour, plus extra for dusting

2 teaspoons baking powder

¼ teaspoon salt

6 tablespoons salted butter, chilled and diced, plus extra for greasing and to serve

½ cup superfine sugar, plus extra for sprinkling

½ cup chopped dried sweetened cranberries

1 egg

⅔ cup buttermilk

finely grated rind of 1 orange

beaten egg white, to glaze

1. Preheat the oven to 400°F. Lightly grease a large baking sheet.

2. Sift together the flour, baking powder, and salt into a large bowl and stir in the butter. Rub the butter in until the mixture resembles fine bread crumbs. Stir in the sugar and most of the cranberries. Beat together the egg, buttermilk, and orange rind and pour into the bowl. Mix to a soft dough. Turn out the dough onto a floured surface and knead gently.

3. Shape and gently pat the dough into an 8½- x 5½-inch rectangle. Use a sharp knife to cut it into six squares. Place the squares on the prepared baking sheet and top with the remaining cranberries, pressing down gently. Lightly brush the tops of the scones with the beaten egg white and sprinkle with sugar.

4. Bake in the preheated oven for 20 minutes, or until risen and golden brown. Transfer to a wire rack to cool, then serve with butter.

2

2
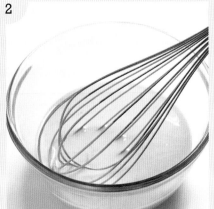

3

COOK'S NOTE
The secret to light, airy, and well risen scones is to handle the dough as gently as possible.

Chocolate & Cinnamon Brownies

 MAKES 16

 PREP TIME:
40 minutes
plus cooling

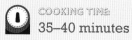 COOKING TIME:
35–40 minutes

nutritional information per cake	348 cal, 19g fat, 9g sat fat, 29g total sugars, 0.3g salt

An all-time favorite, chocolate brownies are really easy to make, keep well, and always taste fantastic. This version is full of pecans, lightly spiced with ground cinnamon, and topped with a sweet white chocolate frosting.

INGREDIENTS

4 ounces semisweet chocolate, broken into pieces

1¾ sticks salted butter, plus extra for greasing

1 cup pecan halves

1¼ cups superfine sugar

4 eggs, beaten

1¾ cups all-purpose flour

2 teaspoons ground cinnamon

2 ounces white chocolate, broken into pieces

2 tablespoons milk

1 cup confectioners' sugar

1. Preheat the oven to 350°F. Grease a shallow 9-inch square cake pan.

2. Melt the semisweet chocolate and 1½ sticks of the butter in a heatproof bowl set over a saucepan of gently simmering water. Remove from the heat and let cool slightly.

3. Set 16 pecan halves to one side for decoration and chop the rest. Beat together the superfine sugar and eggs with an electric mixer until thick and creamy. Then fold in the chocolate mixture, flour, cinnamon, and chopped pecans.

4. Transfer the batter to the prepared pan and bake in the preheated oven for 35–40 minutes, or until just firm to the touch. Let cool in the pan.

5. Melt the remaining butter and white chocolate in a heatproof bowl set over a saucepan of gently simmering water. Remove from the heat and beat in the milk and confectioners' sugar. Spread this mixture over the cooled brownies. Let set for 30 minutes, then cut into 16 squares and top each square with a pecan half.

3

5

5

Chocolate & Cherry Brownies

 MAKES 12    PREP TIME: 30 minutes   COOKING TIME: 45–50 minutes

nutritional information per cake	364 cal, 21g fat, 12g sat fat, 33g total sugars, 0.4g salt

Chunks of sweet white chocolate and juicy fresh cherries make these chocolate brownies extra special.

INGREDIENTS

6 ounces semisweet chocolate, broken into pieces

1½ sticks salted butter, plus extra for greasing

1 cup superfine sugar

3 extra-large eggs, beaten

1 teaspoon vanilla extract

1 cup all-purpose flour

1½ teaspoons baking powder

1 cup pitted fresh cherries

3 ounces white chocolate, coarsely chopped

1. Preheat the oven to 350°F. Grease a shallow 9-inch square baking pan and line with parchment paper.

2. Put the semisweet chocolate and butter into a large, heatproof bowl set over a saucepan of simmering water and heat until melted. Remove from the heat and let cool for 5 minutes.

3. Beat the sugar, eggs, and vanilla extract into the chocolate mixture. Sift in the flour and baking powder and fold in gently. Pour the batter into the prepared pan. Sprinkle with the cherries and the white chocolate.

4. Bake in the preheated oven for 30 minutes. Loosely cover the tops of the brownies with aluminum foil and bake for an additional 15–20 minutes, or until just firm to the touch. Let cool in the pan, then cut into pieces.

2

3

3

GOES WELL WITH
Cut the brownies into small squares and layer in tall sundae glasses with scoops of vanilla ice cream. Top with warm chocolate sauce.

Vanilla Fudge Blondies

 MAKES 9    PREP TIME: 30 minutes    COOKING TIME: 40–45 minutes

nutritional information per cake	428 cal, 22g fat, 10g sat fat, 33g total sugars, 0.5g salt

Similar to brownies in shape and texture but made with chunks of fudge and macadamia nuts instead of chocolate.

INGREDIENTS

1 stick salted butter, softened, plus extra for greasing

1 cup firmly packed, light brown sugar

2 extra-large eggs, beaten

1 teaspoon vanilla extract

2 cups all-purpose flour

1 teaspoon baking powder

4 ounces soft butter fudge, chopped into small pieces

½ cup coarsely chopped macadamia nuts

confectioners' sugar, for dusting

1. Preheat the oven to 350°F. Grease a shallow 8-inch square cake pan and line with parchment paper.

2. Place the butter and brown sugar in a large bowl and beat together until pale and creamy. Gradually beat in the eggs and vanilla extract. Sift the flour and baking powder into the mixture and beat together until well mixed.

3. Add the fudge and chopped nuts and stir together until combined. Spoon the batter into the prepared pan and smooth the surface.

4. Bake in the preheated oven for 40–45 minutes, or until risen and golden brown. Let cool in the pan, then dust with sifted confectioners' sugar to decorate and cut into squares.

FREEZING TIP
Freeze for up to two months, wrapped in foil. Thaw at room temperature for 2-3 hours.

Double Chocolate Pecan Blondies

 MAKES 12    PREP TIME: 30 minutes plus cooling   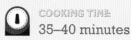 COOKING TIME: 35–40 minutes

nutritional information per cake	346 cal, 21g fat, 9g sat fat, 28g total sugars, 0.25g salt

With chunks of white and dark chocolate and crunchy pecans, these tempting bars are an indulgent treat.

INGREDIENTS

9 ounces white chocolate, broken into pieces

3 tablespoons salted butter, plus extra for greasing

6 ounces semisweet chocolate

2 extra-large eggs, beaten

⅓ cup superfine sugar

1 cup all-purpose flour

1½ teaspoons baking powder

1 cup coarsely chopped pecans

1. Preheat the oven to 350°F. Grease a shallow 8-inch square baking pan.

2. Place 3 ounces of the white chocolate in a heatproof bowl and add the butter. Set the bowl over a saucepan of gently simmering water and heat, stirring occasionally, until melted and smooth. Meanwhile, coarsely chop the remaining white and semisweet chocolate.

3. Beat together the eggs and sugar in a large bowl, then stir in the melted chocolate mixture. Sift the flour and baking powder over the mixture. Add the chopped chocolate and pecans. Mix well.

4. Spoon the batter into the prepared pan and smooth the surface. Bake in the preheated oven for 35–40 minutes, or until golden brown and just firm to the touch in the center. Let stand in the pan until completely cooled and the chocolate chunks inside have set, then invert and cut into pieces.

2

3

4

Vanilla Cake Pops

 MAKES 24

 PREP TIME:
1–1¼ hours
plus chilling

 COOKING TIME:
No cooking

nutritional information per cake	300 cal, 16g fat, 9g sat fat, 28g total sugars, 0.36g salt

These mini "cupcake" cake pops have both child and adult appeal, so they're ideal for a gathering of mixed ages. Once frosted, they'll keep in a cool place for a couple of days.

INGREDIENTS

16 ounces store-bought vanilla cake
⅓ cup mascarpone cheese
½ cup confectioners' sugar
½ teaspoon vanilla extract

decoration
8 ounces milk chocolate, coarsely chopped
24 lollipop sticks
1¼ cups confectioners' sugar
pink food coloring
4 teaspoons cold water
24 small candies, such as mini sugar-coated chocolates
sugar sprinkles

1. Line a baking sheet with parchment paper. Crumble the vanilla cake into a mixing bowl. Add the mascarpone, confectioners' sugar, and vanilla and mix together until you have a thick paste.

2. Divide the paste into 24 pieces. Roll a piece of the paste into a ball. Push this ball into a mini cupcake liner, pressing it down so that when it is removed from the liner you have a mini cupcake shape. Shape the remaining 23 cake pops in the same way. Place on the baking sheet and let chill for 1–2 hours, until firm.

3. Put the chocolate in a heatproof bowl, set the bowl over a saucepan of gently simmering water, and heat until melted. Remove from the heat. Push a lollipop stick into each cake pop. Dip a cake pop into the chocolate, turning it until coated. Lift it from the bowl, letting the excess drip back into the bowl, then place it in a cup or glass. Repeat with the remaining cake pops. Chill or let stand in a cool place until the chocolate has set.

4. Put the confectioners' sugar in a mixing bowl and beat in a dash of pink food coloring and the water until smooth. The icing should almost hold its shape. Spoon a little onto a cake pop, easing it slightly down the sides with the side of a teaspoon. If the icing is too firm, you might need to add a drop more water. Before the icing sets, place a small candy in the center of each cake pop and sprinkle with sugar sprinkles.

Chocolate Mint
Rocky Road Pops

 MAKES 28

 PREP TIME:
1 hour
plus chilling

 COOKING TIME:
No cooking

nutritional information per cake	160 cal, 9g fat, 5g sat fat, 18g total sugars, trace salt

This is a lollipop version of "rocky road," and it is about as easy to make as it gets! The milk chocolate coating has family appeal, but you can use semisweet chocolate instead for a more adult flavor.

INGREDIENTS

10 ounces semisweet chocolate, coarsely chopped

2 tablespoons unsalted butter, softened

1¾ ounces of hard-boiled mint candies

16 ounces milk chocolate

1 cup coarsely chopped mini marshmallows,

28 lollipop sticks

chocolate sprinkles, to decorate

1. Line a baking sheet with parchment paper. Put the semisweet chocolate in a heatproof bowl, set the bowl over a saucepan of gently simmering water, and heat until melted. Stir in the butter. Let stand until the mixture is cool but not beginning to set.

2. Put the mint candies in a plastic food bag and tap firmly with a rolling pin until they are broken into tiny pieces. Finely chop 6 ounces of the milk chocolate, then stir it into the melted semisweet chocolate with the mints and marshmallows until thoroughly mixed.

3. As soon as the mixture is firm enough to hold its shape, divide and roll the mixture into 28 balls. Place them on the baking sheet and chill for 30–60 minutes, or until firm but not brittle. Push a lollipop stick into each cake pop, then chill for 10 minutes.

4. Coarsely chop the remaining milk chocolate and melt as above, then remove from the heat. Dip a cake pop into the chocolate, turning it until coated. Lift it from the bowl, letting the excess drip back into the bowl, and place it in a cup or glass. Sprinkle with chocolate sprinkles. Repeat with the remaining cake pops. Chill or let stand in a cool place until the chocolate has set.

Chewy Marshmallow Bars

 MAKES 10

 PREP TIME:
25 minutes
plus chilling

COOKING TIME:
No cooking

nutritional information per slice	191 cal, 7g fat, 4g sat fat, 17g total sugars, 0.4g salt

These crispy toffee and marshmallow bars are a great treat for children, but adults will love them, too!

INGREDIENTS

3 ounces toffee
4 tablespoons salted butter
2 tablespoons corn syrup
3 cups mini pink and white marshmallows
4 cups crispy rice cereal
2 tablespoons candy-coated chocolates

1. Line a shallow 11 x 7-inch cake pan with parchment paper.

2. Put the toffee, butter, corn syrup, and 2 cups of the marshmallows into a large heatproof bowl set over a saucepan of simmering water. Heat until melted, stirring occasionally.

3. Remove the bowl from the heat. Stir in the rice cereal until thoroughly mixed. Quickly spoon the mixture into the prepared pan and smooth the surface.

4. Scatter with the remaining marshmallows and the chocolates, gently pressing them down. Chill in the refrigerator for about 2 hours, or until firm. Use a sharp knife to cut into 10 bars.

2

3

4

SOMETHING
DIFFERENT
For a chocolate
version, replace
the toffee with
4 ounces milk or
white chocolate,
broken into pieces.

Rocky Road Bars

 MAKES 8

 PREP TIME:
20 minutes
plus chilling

 COOKING TIME:
No cooking

nutritional information per slice	327 cal, 22g fat, 9g sat fat, 23g total sugars, 0.23g salt

Marshmallows, crushed cookies, chocolate, and nuts are the perfect combination for this delicious easy-to-make sweet treat. Stored in an airtight container, the bars will keep for at least one week.

INGREDIENTS

6 ounces milk chocolate or semisweet chocolate

4 tablespoons salted butter

12 shortbread cookies, broken into pieces

1½ cups mini marshmallows

½ cup walnut pieces or peanuts

1. Line a 7-inch square cake pan with parchment paper. Break the chocolate into squares and place in a heatproof bowl set over a saucepan of gently simmering water and heat until melted. Add the butter and stir until melted and combined. Let cool slightly.

2. Stir the broken cookies, marshmallows, and nuts into the chocolate mixture.

3. Pour the mixture into the prepared pan, pressing down with the back of a spoon.

4. Chill in the refrigerator for at least 2 hours, or until firm. Carefully invert out of the pan and cut into eight pieces.

SOMETHING
DIFFERENT
Add some
chopped candied
cherries or dried
apricots for a
fruity flavor.

Date, Pistachio & Honey Slices

 MAKES 12    PREP TIME: 30 minutes   COOKING TIME: 20–25 minutes

nutritional information
per slice   243 cal, 14g fat, 7g sat fat, 11g total sugars, 0.2g salt

A delicious mixture of Mediterranean dates, pistachio nuts, and honey encased in a buttery, crisp pastry.

INGREDIENTS

1¾ cups chopped, pitted dates
2 tablespoons lemon juice
2 tablespoons water
⅔ cup chopped pistachio nuts
2 tablespoons honey
milk, to glaze

pastry dough
1¾ cups all-purpose flour, plus extra for dusting
2 tablespoons superfine sugar
1¼ sticks salted butter
¼–⅓ cup cold water, to mix

1. Place the dates, lemon juice, and water in a saucepan and bring to a boil, stirring. Remove from the heat. Stir in the pistachio nuts and 1 tablespoon of honey. Cover and let cool.

2. Preheat the oven to 400°F. For the pastry, place the flour, sugar, and butter in a food processor and process to fine crumbs. Mix in just enough cold water to bind to a soft, not sticky, dough.

3. Roll out the dough on a floured surface to two 12 x 8-inch rectangles. Place one on a baking sheet. Spread the date-and-nut mixture to within ½ inch of the edge. Top with the remaining dough.

4. Press to seal, trim the edges, and mark into 12 slices. Glaze with the milk. Bake in the preheated oven for 20–25 minutes, or until golden. Brush with the remaining honey and invert onto a wire rack to cool. Cut into slices and serve.

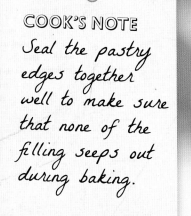

COOK'S NOTE
Seal the pastry edges together well to make sure that none of the filling seeps out during baking.

Vanilla Macaroons

 MAKES 16

 PREP TIME:
20 minutes
plus cooling

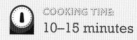 COOKING TIME:
10–15 minutes

nutritional information per cake	125 cal, 5.5g fat, 2g sat fat, 17.5g total sugars, trace salt

Originating from France, these melt-in-the-mouth petits fours are made with almond meal, sugar, and egg whites.

INGREDIENTS

¾ cup almond meal (ground almonds)
1 cup confectioners' sugar
2 extra-large egg whites
¼ cup superfine sugar
½ teaspoon vanilla extract

filling

4 tablespoons unsalted butter, softened
½ teaspoon vanilla extract
1 cup confectioners' sugar, sifted

1. Line two baking sheets with parchment paper. Place the almond meal and confectioners' sugar in a food processor and process for 15 seconds. Sift the mixture into a bowl.

2. Place the egg whites in a clean, grease-free bowl and beat until holding soft peaks. Gradually beat in the superfine sugar to make a firm, glossy meringue. Beat in the vanilla extract.

3. Using a spatula, fold the almond mixture into the meringue one-third at a time. When all the dry ingredients are thoroughly incorporated, continue to cut and fold the mixture until it forms a shiny batter with a thick, ribbonlike consistency.

4. Pour the batter into a pastry bag fitted with a ½-inch plain tip. Pipe 32 small mounds onto the prepared baking sheets. Tap the baking sheets firmly onto a surface to remove air bubbles. Let stand at room temperature for 30 minutes. Preheat the oven to 325°F.

5. Bake in the preheated oven for 10–15 minutes. Cool for 10 minutes, then carefully peel the macaroons off the parchment paper. Let cool completely.

6. To make the filling, beat the butter and vanilla extract in a bowl until pale and fluffy. Gradually beat in the confectioners' sugar until smooth and creamy. Use to sandwich pairs of macaroons together.

3

4

5

Salted Caramel Squares

 MAKES 16

 PREP TIME:
30 minutes
plus chilling

 COOKING TIME:
15 minutes

nutritional information per slice	356 cal, 21g fat, 12g sat fat, 29g total sugars, 0.5g salt

A touch of sea salt added to the caramel gives this sweet treat a modern twist.

INGREDIENTS

1 stick salted butter, softened, plus extra for greasing
¼ cup superfine sugar
1⅓ cups all-purpose flour
½ cup almond meal (ground almonds)

topping
1½ sticks salted butter
½ cup superfine sugar
3 tablespoons corn syrup
1 (14-ounce) can condensed milk
¼ teaspoon sea salt crystals
3 ounces semisweet chocolate, melted

1. Preheat the oven to 350°F. Grease a shallow 8-inch square cake pan.

2. Put the butter and sugar into a bowl and beat together until pale and creamy. Sift in the flour and add the almond meal. Use clean hands to mix and knead to a crumbly dough. Press into the bottom of the prepared pan and prick the surface all over with a fork. Bake in the preheated oven for 15 minutes, or until pale golden. Let cool.

3. To make the topping, put the butter, sugar, corn syrup, and condensed milk into a saucepan over low heat and heat gently until the sugar has dissolved. Increase the heat to medium, bring to a boil, then simmer for 6–8 minutes, stirring continuously, until the mixture becomes thick. Stir in half the salt, then quickly pour the caramel over the shortbread crust. Sprinkle over the remaining salt.

4. Spoon the chocolate into a paper pastry bag and snip off the end. Pipe the chocolate over the caramel and swirl with the tip of a knife. Let cool, then chill for 2 hours, or until firm. Cut into 16 squares.

2

3

4

COOK'S NOTE
A heavy saucepan is essential for making the caramel and you must stir the mixture continuously to prevent it from burning.

Chocolate Fudge

 MAKES
32 pieces

 PREP TIME:
20 minutes
plus setting

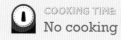 COOKING TIME:
No cooking

nutritional information per piece	195 cal, 9g fat, 3.5g sat fat, 28g total sugars, 0.16g salt

Everyone loves fudge, and this version with chocolate and nuts is a real winner. Serve as an after-dinner treat with coffee.

INGREDIENTS

2 tablespoons unsweetened cocoa powder

1¼ cups whole milk

4 ounces bittersweet chocolate, at least 85 percent cocoa solids, finely chopped

4 cups superfine sugar

1 stick salted butter, chopped, plus extra for greasing

pinch of salt

1½ teaspoons vanilla extract

1½ cups chopped pecans, walnuts, or toasted hazelnuts, or a mixture of nuts

1. Put the cocoa powder into a small bowl, add 2 tablespoons of the milk, and stir until blended. Pour the remaining milk into a large, heavy saucepan, then add the cocoa mixture and chocolate and simmer over medium–high heat, stirring, until the chocolate melts. Add the sugar, butter, and salt, reduce the heat to low, and stir until the butter is melted, the sugar is dissolved, and you can't feel any of the grains when you rub a spoon against the side of the pan.

2. Increase the heat and bring the milk to a boil. Cover the pan and boil for 2 minutes, then uncover and carefully clip a sugar thermometer to the side. Continue boiling, without stirring, until the temperature reaches 239°F, or until a small amount of the mixture forms a soft ball when dropped in cold water.

3. Meanwhile, line an 8-inch square cake pan with aluminum foil, grease the foil, then set aside.

4. Remove the pan from the heat, stir in the vanilla extract, and beat the fudge until it thickens. Stir in the nuts.

5. Pour the fudge mixture into the prepared pan and use a wet spatula to smooth the surface. Set aside and let stand for at least 2 hours to become firm. Lift the fudge out of the pan, then peel off the foil. Cut the fudge into eight 1-inch strips, then cut each strip into four pieces. Store the fudge for up to one week in an airtight container.

Coconut & Raspberry Squares

 MAKES 9  PREP TIME: 25 minutes  COOKING TIME: 35–45 minutes

nutritional information per slice	351 cal, 18g fat, 12g sat fat, 28g total sugars, 0.3g salt

These scrumptious squares have a buttery shortbread crust and a chewy coconut meringue.

INGREDIENTS

1¼ sticks salted butter, softened, plus extra for greasing
⅓ cup superfine sugar
1 extra-large egg yolk
1⅔ cups all-purpose flour
⅓ cup seedless raspberry preserves
unsweetened cocoa powder, to dust (optional)

coconut topping
2 extra-large egg whites
¼ cup superfine sugar
½ cup dry unsweetened coconut

1. Preheat the oven to 350°F. Grease a shallow 9-inch square cake pan.

2. Beat together the butter and sugar in a large bowl until fluffy. Beat in the egg yolk, then sift in the flour and mix to a soft dough. Knead lightly, then press into the bottom of the prepared pan. Prick all over with a fork and bake in the preheated oven for 20–25 minutes, or until pale golden.

3. To make the topping, put the egg whites into a large bowl and beat until it holds stiff peaks. Gradually beat in the sugar to make a firm, glossy meringue. Fold in two-thirds of the coconut. Spread the preserves over the cooked crust in the pan, then spoon the meringue over the preserves. Sprinkle with the remaining coconut.

4. Return to the oven for 15–20 minutes, or until the meringue topping is crisp and golden. Let cool in the pan, then dust with cooca powder, if using, and cut into nine squares.

2

3

3

Apricot Oat Bars

 MAKES 10    PREP TIME: 15 minutes    COOKING TIME: 20–25 minutes

nutritional information per slice	296 cal, 17g fat, 3.5g sat fat, 18g total sugars, 0.3g salt

Oat bars are really easy to make and taste so much better than store-bought cakes. Great for lunch bags or fiber-packed snacks, this version is flavored with apricots, honey, and sesame seeds.

INGREDIENTS

1½ sticks margarine, plus extra for greasing

⅓ cup demerara sugar or other raw sugar

¼ cup honey

1 cup chopped dried apricots

2 teaspoons sesame seeds

2½ cups rolled oats

1. Preheat the oven to 350°F. Grease a shallow 10½ x 6½-inch baking pan.

2. Put the margarine, sugar, and honey into a small saucepan over low heat and heat until the ingredients have melted together—do not boil. When the ingredients are well combined, stir in the apricots, sesame seeds, and oats.

3. Spoon the mixture into the prepared pan and smooth the surface with the back of a spoon. Bake in the preheated oven for 20–25 minutes, or until golden brown.

4. Remove from the oven, cut into 10 bars, and let cool completely before removing from the pan.

COOK'S NOTE
Oat bars are still
soft when they
come out of the oven—
they set on cooling.

Ginger & Chocolate
Oat Bars

 MAKES 12

 PREP TIME:
15 minutes
plus chilling

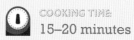 COOKING TIME:
15–20 minutes

nutritional information per slice	388 cal, 22g fat, 12g sat fat, 24g total sugars, 0.3g salt

Spicy preserved ginger and a rich chocolate glaze add an extra special twist to these bars.

INGREDIENTS

1½ sticks salted butter, plus extra for greasing

½ cup firmly packed light brown sugar

3 tablespoons corn syrup

1 tablespoon preserved ginger syrup

2 pieces preserved ginger, finely chopped

3¾ cups rolled oats

chocolate glaze

6 ounces semisweet chocolate, broken into pieces

3 tablespoons salted butter

1. Preheat the oven to 350°F. Grease a shallow 11 x 7-inch baking pan.

2. Put the butter, sugar, corn syrup, and preserved ginger syrup into a large saucepan over low heat and heat gently until melted. Remove from the heat and stir in the chopped ginger and oats.

3. Spoon the mixture into the prepared pan and smooth the surface. Bake in the preheated oven for 15–20 minutes, or until pale golden. Let cool in the pan.

4. To make the glaze, put the chocolate and butter into a heatproof bowl set over a saucepan of simmering water and heat until melted. Stir until smooth, then spread over the cooled oat bars. Chill in the refrigerator for 1 hour, or until set. Cut into 12 bars.

Raisin Oat Bars

 MAKES 14   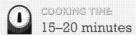 PREP TIME: 15 minutes   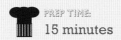 COOKING TIME: 15–20 minutes

nutritional information per slice	147 cal, 8g fat, 5g sat fat, 12g total sugars, 0.15g salt

These simple oat bars have a sweet buttery flavor and are studded with juicy raisins. You can replace the raisins with golden raisins or dried currants or try milk or semisweet chocolate chips instead.

INGREDIENTS

1½ cups rolled oats

½ cup demerara sugar or other raw sugar

½ cup raisins

1 stick salted butter, melted, plus extra for greasing

1. Preheat the oven to 375°F. Grease a shallow 11 x 7-inch baking pan.

2. Combine the oats, sugar, and raisins with the butter in a mixing bowl, stirring well. Spoon the mixture into the prepared pan and press down firmly with the back of a spoon. Bake in the preheated oven for 15–20 minutes, or until golden.

3. Using a sharp knife, mark into 14 bars, then let cool in the pan for 10 minutes. Carefully transfer the bars to a wire rack to cool completely.

2

2

3

Cookies

Chocolate Chip Cookies

 MAKES 8    PREP TIME:
10 minutes   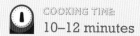 COOKING TIME:
10–12 minutes

nutritional information per cookie	353 cal, 19g fat, 6g sat fat, 27g total sugars, 0.5g salt

These traditional chocolate-laden cookies are crisp on the outside and chewy in the middle. Delicious warm from the oven, they also keep well stored in an airtight container.

INGREDIENTS

unsalted butter, melted,
for greasing
1⅓ cups all-purpose flour, sifted
1 teaspoon baking powder
1 stick margarine, melted
⅓ cup firmly packed
light brown sugar
¼ cup superfine sugar
½ teaspoon vanilla extract
1 egg, beaten
¾ cup semisweet chocolate chips

1. Preheat the oven to 375°F. Lightly grease two baking sheets.

2. Place all of the ingredients in a large mixing bowl and beat until well combined.

3. Place tablespoons of the dough on the prepared baking sheets, spaced well apart.

4. Bake in the preheated oven for 10–12 minutes, or until golden brown. Transfer to a wire rack and let cool.

1

2

3

SOMETHING DIFFERENT
Add some coarsely
chopped nuts to the
cookie dough—try
pecans, hazelnuts,
or blanched almonds.

Classic Oatmeal Cookies

 MAKES 30    PREP TIME: 15 minutes   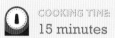 COOKING TIME: 15 minutes

nutritional information per cookie	141 cal, 6g fat, 3g sat fat, 9g total sugars, 0.3g salt

These simple cookies are made from pantry ingredients and take minutes to make and bake.

INGREDIENTS

1½ sticks salted butter, softened, plus extra for greasing

1⅓ cups demerara sugar or other raw sugar

1 egg, beaten

¼ cup water

1 teaspoon vanilla extract

4 cups rolled oats

1 cup all-purpose flour

1 teaspoon salt

½ teaspoon baking soda

1. Preheat the oven to 350°F. Grease two large baking sheets.

2. Place the butter and sugar in a large bowl and beat together until pale and creamy. Beat in the egg, water, and vanilla extract until the mixture is smooth. Mix together the oats, flour, salt, and baking soda in a separate bowl, then gradually stir the oat mixture into the creamed mixture until thoroughly combined.

3. Place tablespoonfuls of the dough on the prepared baking sheets, spaced well apart.

4. Bake in the preheated oven for 15 minutes, or until golden brown. Transfer to a wire rack to cool completely.

COOK'S NOTE
To get even cookies, use a small ice cream scoop to measure out the dough.

Black & White Cookies

 MAKES 20

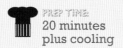 PREP TIME:
20 minutes
plus cooling

 COOKING TIME:
15 minutes

nutritional information
per cookie

240 cal, 11g fat, 6.5g sat fat, 23g total sugars, trace salt

*Crisp and buttery vanilla-flavored cookies with a
striking decoration of creamy icing and melted chocolate.*

INGREDIENTS

1 stick unsalted butter, softened,
plus extra for greasing
1 teaspoon vanilla extract
1 cup superfine sugar
2 eggs, beaten
2⅓ cups all-purpose flour
½ teaspoon baking powder
1 cup whole milk

icing

1¾ cups confectioners' sugar
½ cup heavy cream
⅛ teaspoon vanilla extract
3 ounces semisweet chocolate,
broken into pieces

1. Preheat the oven to 375°F. Grease three baking sheets. Place the butter, vanilla extract, and superfine sugar in a large bowl. Beat the mixture with an electric mixer until light and fluffy, then beat in the eggs a bit at a time.

2. Sift the flour and baking powder and fold into the creamed mixture, loosening with milk a little at a time until both are used up and the dough is a dropping consistency. Drop heaping tablespoonfuls of the dough, spaced well apart, on the prepared baking sheets. Bake in the preheated oven for 15 minutes, or until turning golden at the edges and light to the touch. Transfer to wire racks to cool completely.

3. To make the icing, put the confectioners' sugar in a bowl and mix in half the cream and the vanilla extract. The consistency should be thick but spreadable. Using a spatula, spread half of each cookie with white icing. Now, melt the chocolate in a bowl over a saucepan of simmering water. Remove from the heat and stir in the remaining cream. Spread the dark icing over the uncoated cookie halves.

1

2

3

GOES WELL WITH *These are delicious with a mid morning cup of coffee.*

Snickerdoodles

 MAKES 24

 PREP TIME:
20 minutes

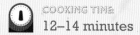 COOKING TIME:
12–14 minutes

nutritional information per cookie	102 cal, 3.5g fat, 2g sat fat, 9g total sugars, 0.2g salt

These crisp and buttery cookies have a wonderful cinnamon-sugar coating.

INGREDIENTS

6 tablespoons salted butter, softened
1 cup superfine sugar
1 extra-large egg, beaten
½ teaspoon vanilla extract
2 cups all-purpose flour
1 teaspoon baking powder
3 tablespoons granulated sugar
1 tablespoon ground cinnamon

1. Preheat the oven to 350°F. Line two large baking sheets with parchment paper.

2. Put the butter and superfine sugar into a bowl and beat together until pale and creamy. Gradually beat in the egg and vanilla extract. Sift together the flour and baking powder and stir into the bowl. Mix to a smooth dough.

3. Mix together the granulated sugar and cinnamon on a plate. Divide the dough into 24 even pieces and shape each piece into a walnut-size ball. Roll the balls in the cinnamon sugar, then place on the prepared baking sheets, spaced well apart to allow for spreading. Flatten each ball slightly with your fingers.

4. Bake in the preheated oven for 12–14 minutes, or until golden. Let cool on the baking sheets for 5 minutes, then transfer to a wire rack to cool completely.

2

3

4

SOMETHING
DIFFERENT
Replace 2
tablespoons flour
with unsweetened
cocoa powder and
add 1 teaspoonful
instant coffee
powder to the
cinnamon coating.

Coconut & Cranberry Cookies

 MAKES 30

 PREP TIME: 10 minutes

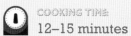 COOKING TIME: 12–15 minutes

nutritional information per cookie	123 cal, 7g fat, 5g sat fat, 5g total sugars, 0.2g salt

Naturally sweet coconut complements the sharpness of the dried cranberries perfectly in these crumbly cookies.

INGREDIENTS

2 sticks salted butter, softened
⅔ cup superfine sugar
1 egg yolk
2 teaspoons vanilla extract
2¼ cups all-purpose flour
pinch of salt
½ cup dry unsweetened coconut
¼ cup dried cranberries

1. Preheat the oven to 375°F. Line several baking sheets with parchment paper.

2. Put the butter and sugar into a bowl and beat together until pale and creamy, then beat in the egg yolk and vanilla extract. Sift together the flour and salt into the mixture, add the coconut and cranberries, and stir until thoroughly combined.

3. Scoop up tablespoons of the dough and place in mounds on the prepared baking sheets, spaced well apart.

4. Bake in the preheated oven for 12–15 minutes, or until golden brown. Let cool on the baking sheets for 5–10 minutes, then, using a spatula, transfer to wire racks to cool completely.

2

2

3

FREEZING TIP
Freeze the
cookies for up
to one month.
Thaw at room
temperature for
1-2 hours.

Chocolate Mint Cookies

 MAKES 15

 PREP TIME:
25 minutes
plus chilling

 COOKING TIME:
10–15 minutes

nutritional information per cookie	293 cal, 17g fat, 10g sat fat, 21g total sugars, 0.4g salt

These luxurious chocolate cookies have a wonderful minty middle and are just perfect to serve with coffee after a special meal.

INGREDIENTS

2 sticks salted butter, softened

⅔ cup superfine sugar

1 egg yolk, lightly beaten

2 teaspoons vanilla extract

2 cups all-purpose flour

¼ cup unsweetend cocoa powder

pinch of salt

¼ cup finely chopped candied cherries

15 after-dinner mint thins

chocolate topping

4 ounces semisweet chocolate, broken into pieces

2 ounces white chocolate, broken into pieces

1. Put the butter and sugar into a bowl and beat together until pale and creamy, then beat in the egg yolk and vanilla extract. Sift together the flour, cocoa powder, and salt into the mixture, add the cherries, and stir until thoroughly combined. Halve the dough, shape into balls, wrap in plastic wrap, and chill in the refrigerator for 30–60 minutes.

2. Preheat the oven to 375°F. Line two baking sheets with parchment paper. Unwrap the dough and roll out between two sheets of parchment paper. Stamp out 30 cookies with a 2½-inch plain square cutter and place on the prepared baking sheets, spaced well apart. Bake in the preheated oven for 10–15 minutes, or until firm. Immediately place an after-dinner mint on top of half of the cookies, then cover with the remaining cookies. Press down gently and let cool on the baking sheets.

3. Melt the semisweet chocolate in a heatproof bowl set over a saucepan of gently simmering water and let cool. Put the cookies on a wire rack, spoon the semisweet chocolate over them. and let set. Melt the white chocolate in a heatproof bowl set over a saucepan of barely simmering water then let cool. Drizzle over the cookies. Let set.

Eggnog Cookies

 MAKES 35    PREP TIME: 20 minutes plus cooling    COOKING TIME: 20–25 minutes

nutritional information per cookie	112 cal, 4g fat, 2.5g sat fat, 10g total sugars, 0.1g salt

Flavored with rum, vanilla, and nutmeg, these wonderfully crisp and golden cookies are definitely for only the grown-ups!

INGREDIENTS

1 egg, beaten
1 cup superfine sugar
⅓ cup rum
3 tablespoons milk
1¼ sticks salted butter plus
1 tablespoon, softened,
plus extra for greasing
1 teaspoon vanilla extract
2 egg yolks
2¼ cups all-purpose flour
1 teaspoon baking powder
¾ teaspoon ground nutmeg
1⅓ cups confectioners' sugar

1. Preheat the oven to 325°F. Grease several baking sheets. To make the rum mixture, beat together the egg, 2 tablespoons of the superfine sugar, rum, and milk until frothy. Set aside.

2. In a large bowl, beat together the rest of the superfine sugar and 1¼ sticks of the butter until pale and creamy. Beat in the vanilla extract and egg yolks until smooth.

3. Sift together the flour, baking powder, and ½ teaspoon of nutmeg into the mixture and beat in ½ cup of the rum-and-milk mixture until just combined.

4. Place heaping teaspoonfuls of the dough on the prepared baking sheets, spaced well apart. Flatten slightly with damp fingers and bake in the preheated oven for 20–25 minutes, or until the bottom of the cookies turn golden.

5. Let cool for 5 minutes on the baking sheets and then transfer to wire racks to cool completely.

6. Once the cookies are cool, beat together the confectioners' sugar, remaining 1 tablespoon of butter, and the remaining rum-and-milk mixture to make a soft, spreadable frosting. Frost the cookies and sprinkle over the remaining nutmeg. Let set for a few hours.

Giant Chocolate Chunk Cookies

MAKES 12   PREP TIME: 10 minutes   COOKING TIME: 15–20 minutes

nutritional information per cookie	376 cal, 17g fat, 10g sat fat, 34g total sugars, 0.5g salt

Chocolate chunks melt into the vanilla dough during baking to produce a lovely sweet flavor and chewy texture.

INGREDIENTS

1 stick salted butter, softened

⅔ cup superfine sugar

½ cup firmly packed light brown sugar

2 extra-large eggs, lightly beaten

1 teaspoon vanilla extract

2¼ cups all-purpose flour

1 teaspoon baking soda

10 ounces chocolate chunks

1. Preheat the oven to 350°F. Line three to four large baking sheets with parchment paper.

2. Place the butter and sugars in a large bowl and beat together until pale and creamy. Beat the eggs and vanilla extract into the mixture until smooth. Sift in the flour and baking soda and beat together until well mixed. Stir in the chocolate chunks.

3. Drop 12 large spoonfuls of the dough onto the prepared baking sheets, spaced well apart.

4. Bake in the preheated oven for 15–20 minutes, or until set and golden brown. Let cool on the baking sheets for 2–3 minutes, then transfer the cookies to a wire rack to cool completely.

2

2

3

COOK'S NOTE
Because of their size, cook only three to four cookies at a time on a baking sheet.

Apple & Oatmeal Cookies

 MAKES 26    PREP TIME: 20 minutes    COOKING TIME: 12–15 minutes

nutritional information **per cookie** : 160 cal, 8g fat, 5g sat fat, 11g total sugars, 0.3g salt

Chunks of sweet apple, oats, and raisins combine to make these moist and crumbly cookies.

INGREDIENTS

2 large apples, such as Pippin, peeled and cored

1 teaspoon lemon juice

2 sticks salted butter, softened, plus extra for greasing

½ cup firmly packed light brown sugar

½ cup superfine sugar

1 egg, beaten

1¾ cups all-purpose flour

2¾ teaspoons baking powder

1⅔ cups rolled oats

½ cup raisins

1. Preheat the oven to 350°F. Grease three large baking sheets. Finely dice the apples and toss in the lemon juice.

2. Place the butter, brown sugar, and superfine sugar in a bowl and beat together until creamy. Gradually beat in the egg. Sift in the flour and baking powder and add the oats, raisins, and apple. Mix until thoroughly combined.

3. Place tablespoonsful of the dough on the prepared baking sheets, spaced well apart.

4. Bake in the preheated oven for 12–15 minutes, or until golden around the edges. Let cool on the baking sheets for 5–10 minutes, or until firm enough to transfer to a wire rack to cool completely.

FREEZING TIP
Open freeze on baking sheets until solid, pack into freezer bags, and freeze for up to two months. Thaw at room temperature for an hour.

Cappuccino Cookies

 MAKES 30

 PREP TIME:
30 minutes
plus chilling

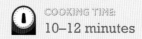 COOKING TIME:
10–12 minutes

nutritional information per cookie	143 cal, 8g fat, 5g sat fat, 8g total sugars, 0.2g salt

Smothered in creamy white chocolate and dusted with cocoa powder, these crisp cookies taste divine and are the perfect accompaniment to a hot mug of coffee.

INGREDIENTS

2 envelopes instant cappuccino
1 tablespoon hot water
2 sticks salted butter, softened
⅔ cup superfine sugar
1 egg yolk, lightly beaten
2¼ cups all-purpose flour
pinch of salt

to decorate
6 ounces white chocolate, broken into pieces
unsweetened cocoa powder, for dusting

1. Empty the cappuccino envelopes into a small bowl and stir in the hot, but not boiling, water to make a paste. Put the butter and sugar into a bowl and beat together until pale and creamy, then beat in the egg yolk and cappuccino paste. Sift together the flour and salt into the mixture and stir until thoroughly combined. Halve the dough, shape into balls, wrap in plastic wrap, and chill in the refrigerator for 30–60 minutes.

2. Preheat the oven to 375°F. Line two baking sheets with parchment paper. Unwrap the dough and roll out between two sheets of parchment paper. Stamp out cookies with a 2½-inch round cutter and put them on the prepared baking sheets, spaced well apart.

3. Bake in the preheated oven for 10–12 minutes, or until golden brown. Let cool for 5-10 minutes, then transfer to wire racks to cool completely. When the cookies are cool, place the wire racks over a sheet of parchment paper. Put the chocolate into a heatproof bowl and melt over a saucepan of gently simmering water. Remove the bowl from the heat and let cool, then spoon the chocolate over the cookies. Gently tap the wire racks to level the surface and let set. Dust lightly with cocoa powder.

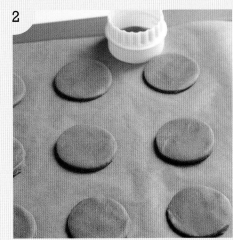

Icebox Cookies

 MAKES 56

 PREP TIME:
20 minutes
plus chilling

 COOKING TIME:
12 minutes

nutritional information per cookie	44 cal, 2g fat, 1g sat fat, 2g total sugars, 0.1g salt

Great for unexpected guests or hungry kids home from school, this cookie dough can be sliced and baked straight from the freezer!

INGREDIENTS

2⅔ cups all-purpose flour

2 tablespoons unsweetened cocoa powder

½ teaspoon baking soda

1 teaspoon ground ginger

½ teaspoon ground cinnamon

½ cup dark molasses

¼ cup boiling water

1 stick salted butter, softened

¼ cup superfine sugar

confectioners' sugar, for dusting

1. Sift together the flour, cocoa powder, baking soda, ginger, and cinnamon into a bowl, then set aside. Mix the molasses with the water and set aside.

2. Put the butter into a large bowl and beat with an electric mixer until creamy. Slowly add the superfine sugar and continue beating until light and fluffy. Gradually add the flour mixture, alternating it with the molasses mixture to form a soft dough.

3. Scrape equal amounts of the dough onto two pieces of plastic wrap and roll into logs, using the plastic wrap as a guide, each about 7½ inches long and 1½ inches thick. Put the dough logs in the refrigerator for 2 hours, then transfer to the freezer for at least 2 hours and up to 2 months.

4. When ready to bake, preheat the oven to 350°F and line one or two baking sheets, depending on how many cookies you are baking, with parchment paper. Unwrap the dough logs, trim the ends, and cut into ¼-inch slices. Rewrap any unused dough and return to the freezer.

5. Place the dough slices on the prepared baking sheet(s) and bake in the preheated oven for 12 minutes. Remove from the oven, let cool on the sheet(s) for 3 minutes, then transfer to wire racks, dust with confectioners' sugar, and let cool completely.

1

2

3

Cinnamon Stars

 MAKES 20

 PREP TIME:
25 minutes
plus chilling

 COOKING TIME:
25 minutes

nutritional information per cookie	116 cal, 8g fat, 0.6g sat fat, 9g total sugars, trace salt

These beautiful little spiced hazelnut star cookies are perfect to give as a homemade Christmas gift.

INGREDIENTS

2 egg whites
1⅓ cups confectioners' sugar, plus extra for dusting
3 cups ground hazelnuts, roasted
1 tablespoon ground cinnamon

1. Beat the egg whites in a clean, grease-free bowl until stiff. Stir in the sugar until thoroughly combined, then continue to beat until thick and glossy.

2. Remove ¼ cup of this mixture and set aside. Then fold the hazelnuts and cinnamon into the remaining mixture to make a stiff dough. Chill in the refrigerator for about an hour.

3. Preheat the oven to 275°F. Line two baking sheets with parchment paper. Roll out the dough to ½ inch thick on a surface amply dusted with confectioners' sugar.

4. Cut the dough into shapes, using a 2-inch star-shape cutter, dusting with confectioners' sugar to prevent the dough from sticking. Reroll as necessary until all of the mixture is used.

5. Place the cookies on the prepared baking sheets, spaced well apart, and spread the top of each star with the reserved egg white icing.

6. Bake in the preheated oven for 25 minutes, or until the cookies are still white and crisp on top but slightly soft and moist underneath. Turn off the oven and open the oven door to release the heat and dry the cookies out in the oven for 10 more minutes. Transfer to wire racks to cool completely.

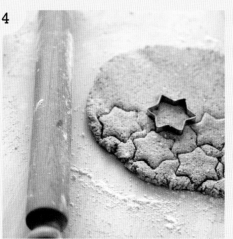

White Chocolate & Macadamia Nut Cookies

  MAKES 16

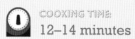 PREP TIME: 25 minutes

COOKING TIME: 12–14 minutes

nutritional information per cookie	165 cal, 10g fat, 5g sat fat, 10g total sugars, 0.2g salt

These chunky choc and nut cookies are so quick and easy to make, they'll soon become a family favorite!

INGREDIENTS

1 stick salted butter, softened, plus extra for greasing

½ cup firmly packed light brown sugar

1 tablespoon corn syrup

1⅓ cups all-purpose flour

2 teaspoons baking powder

⅓ cup coarsely chopped macadamia nuts

2 ounces white chocolate, chopped into chunks

1. Preheat the oven to 350°F. Grease two large baking sheets.

2. Put the butter and sugar into a bowl and beat together until pale and creamy, then beat in the corn syrup. Sift in the flour and baking powder, add the nuts, and mix to form a rough dough.

3. Divide the dough into 16 even balls and place on the prepared baking sheets, spaced well apart to allow for spreading. Slightly flatten each ball with your fingertips and top with the chocolate chunks, pressing them lightly into the dough.

4. Bake in the preheated oven for 12–14 minutes, or until just set and pale golden. Let cool on the baking sheets for 5 minutes, then transfer to a wire rack to cool completely.

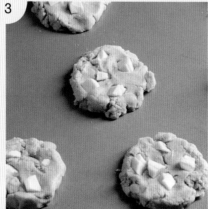

COOK'S NOTE
If the cookies have spread during baking, reshape them with a knife when they come out of the oven.

Marshmallow S'mores

 MAKES 15    PREP TIME: 30 minutes plus chilling   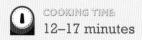 COOKING TIME: 12–17 minutes

nutritional information per cookie	371 cal, 20g fat, 12g sat fat, 30g total sugars, 0.4g salt

The name s'mores is a shortened version of "some more"—and everyone will want more of these chocolate cookies with a marshmallow filling!

INGREDIENTS

2 sticks salted butter, softened

⅔ cup superfine sugar

2 teaspoons finely grated orange rind

1 egg yolk, lightly beaten

2 cups all-purpose flour

¼ cup unsweetened cocoa powder

½ teaspoon ground cinnamon

pinch of salt

30 yellow marshmallows, halved horizontally

10 ounces semisweet chocolate, broken into pieces

¼ cup orange marmalade

15 walnut halves, to decorate

1. Place the butter, sugar, and orange rind in a large bowl and beat together until light and fluffy, then beat in the egg yolk. Sift together the flour, cocoa, cinnamon, and salt into the mixture and stir until combined. Halve the dough, shape into balls, wrap in plastic wrap, and chill in the refrigerator for 30–60 minutes.

2. Preheat the oven to 375°F. Line several large baking sheets with parchment paper. Unwrap the dough and roll out between two sheets of parchment paper. Cut out 30 cookies with a 2½-inch fluted round cutter and place them on the prepared baking sheets, spaced well apart. Bake in the preheated oven for 10–15 minutes. Let cool for 5 minutes. Turn half of the cookies upside down and put four marshmallow halves on each of the turned-over cookies. Bake these marshmallow-topped cookies with for an additional 1–2 minutes. Let all the cookies cool on wire racks for 30 minutes.

3. Place the chocolate in a heatproof bowl, set the bowl over a saucepan of gently simmering water, and heat until melted. Line a baking sheet with parchment paper. Spread the marmalade over the undersides of the uncovered cookies and place them on top of the marshmallow-covered cookies. Dip the cookies in the melted chocolate to coat. Place a walnut half in the center of each cookie and let set.

1

2

3

Gift Cookies

 MAKES 30

 PREP TIME:
30 minutes
plus chilling

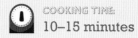 COOKING TIME:
10–15 minutes

nutritional information **per cookie**	140 cal, 7g fat, 4g sat fat, 12g total sugars, 0.2g salt

Perfect for a Christmas treat or gift, these holly- and star-shape, orange-flavor cookies are delicately piped with letters of the alphabet.

INGREDIENTS

2 sticks salted butter, softened
⅔ cup superfine sugar
1 egg yolk, lightly beaten
2 teaspoons orange juice or orange liqueur
finely grated rind of 1 orange
2¼ cups all-purpose flour
pinch of salt

to decorate
1 egg white
1¾ cups confectioners' sugar
few drops each of 2 food colorings
edible silver balls

1. Place the butter and superfine sugar in a large bowl and beat together until pale and creamy, then beat in the egg yolk, orange juice, and grated rind. Sift together the flour and salt into the mixture and stir until combined. Halve the dough, shape into balls, wrap in plastic wrap, and chill in the refrigerator for 30–60 minutes.

2. Preheat the oven to 375°F. Line two large baking sheets with parchment paper. Unwrap the dough and roll out to ⅛ inch thick. Cut out star and holly shapes with cookie cutters and place them on the prepared baking sheets, spaced well apart. Bake in the preheated oven for 10–15 minutes, or until light golden brown.

3. Let cool on the baking sheets for 5–10 minutes, then transfer to wire racks to cool completely.

4. Leave the cookies on the racks. Put the egg white and confectioners' sugar into a bowl and beat until smooth, adding a little water, if necessary. Transfer half the icing to another bowl and color each bowl with a different color. Put both icings in pastry bags with fine tips and use to decorate the cookies and write the initials of the person who will receive the cookies as a gift. Finish with silver balls and let set.

Butterscotch Cookies

 MAKES 22  PREP TIME: 20 minutes  COOKING TIME: 8–10 minutes

nutritional information
per cookie

118 cal, 5.5g fat, 3g sat fat, 9.5g total sugars, 0.35g salt

Chunks of melted toffee give these golden brown cookies a deliciously chewy texture.

INGREDIENTS

¾ cup firmly packed
light brown sugar

1 stick salted butter, softened

1 extra-large egg, beaten

1 teaspoon vanilla extract

1⅔ cups all-purpose flour

1 teaspoon baking soda

2¼ teaspoons baking powder

10 toffees, chopped

1. Preheat the oven to 350°F. Line three large baking sheets with parchment paper.

2. Put the sugar and butter into a bowl and beat together until creamy. Beat in the egg and vanilla extract. Sift together the flour, baking soda, and baking powder and stir in thoroughly. Stir in the toffees.

3. Place walnut-size spoonfuls of the dough on the prepared baking sheets, spaced well apart.

4. Bake in the preheated oven for 8–10 minutes, or until light golden brown. Let cool on the baking sheets, then peel away from the parchment paper.

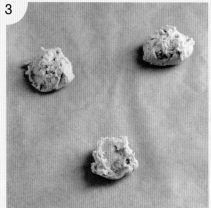

COOK'S NOTE
Let the toffees
stand in a warm
place for about
30 minutes
before chopping
so they soften
up a little.

Gingersnaps

 MAKES 30   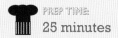 PREP TIME: 25 minutes   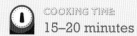 COOKING TIME: 15–20 minutes

nutritional information per cookie	107 cal, 4g fat, 2.5g sat fat, 9g total sugars, 0.3g salt

These are traditional British cookies with a wonderful crisp texture and warming ginger flavor–perfect with a hot drink!

INGREDIENTS

2¾ cups all-purpose flour
1 teaspoon baking soda
4 teaspoons baking powder
pinch of salt
1 cup superfine sugar
1 tablespoon ground ginger
1 stick salted butter,
plus extra for greasing
⅓ cup corn syrup
1 egg, beaten
1 teaspoon grated orange rind

1. Preheat the oven to 325°F. Lightly grease several baking sheets.

2. Sift together the flour, baking soda, baking powder, salt, sugar, and ginger into a large mixing bowl.

3. Heat together the butter and corn syrup in a saucepan over low heat until the butter has melted. Remove the pan from the heat and let cool slightly, then pour the contents onto the dry ingredients.

4. Add the egg and orange rind and mix thoroughly with a wooden spoon to form a dough. Using your hands, carefully shape the dough into 30 even balls. Place the balls on the prepared baking sheets, spaced well apart, then flatten them slightly with your fingers.

5. Bake in the preheated oven for 15–20 minutes, then carefully transfer to a wire rack to cool completely.

Sugar Cookies

  MAKES 20 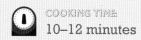 PREP TIME: 20 minutes plus chilling COOKING TIME 10–12 minutes

nutritional information per cookie | 90 cal, 5g fat, 3g sat fat, 3g total sugars, trace salt

Crisp, light, and buttery with a hint of lemon and a sweet sugary coating—the perfect cookie!

INGREDIENTS

1 stick salted butter, softened, plus extra for greasing

¼ cup superfine sugar, plus extra for sprinkling

1 teaspoon finely grated lemon rind

1 egg yolk

1⅓ cups all-purpose flour, plus extra for dusting

1. Place the butter and sugar in a bowl and beat together until pale and creamy. Beat in the lemon rind and egg yolk. Sift in the flour and mix to a soft dough. Turn out onto a floured surface and knead until smooth, adding a little more flour, if necessary. Halve the dough, shape into balls, wrap in plastic wrap, and chill in the refrigerator for 1 hour.

2. Preheat the oven to 350°F. Lightly grease two large baking sheets.

3. Roll out the dough on a lightly floured surface to a thickness of ¼ inch. Using 2¾-inch flower-shape and heart-shape cutters, stamp out 20 cookies, rerolling the dough as necessary. Place on the prepared baking sheets and sprinkle with sugar.

4. Bake in the preheated oven for 10–12 minutes, or until pale golden. Let cool on the baking sheets for 2–3 minutes, then transfer to a wire rack to cool completely.

1

3

3

Snowflake Gingerbread

 MAKES 30

 PREP TIME:
25 minutes
plus cooling

 COOKING TIME:
10 minutes

nutritional information per cookie	111 cal, 3.5g fat, 2g sat fat, 11g total sugars, 0.2g salt

These festive cookies can be made a couple of weeks before Christmas. Place in boxes lined with tissue or cellophane bags to give as presents.

INGREDIENTS

2¾ cups all-purpose flour, plus extra for dusting
1 tablespoon ground ginger
1 teaspoon baking soda
1 stick salted butter, softened, plus extra for greasing
¾ cup firmly packed light brown sugar
1 egg, beaten
¼ cup corn syrup

icing
1 cup confectioners' sugar
2 tablespoons lemon juice

1. Preheat the oven to 350°F. Grease three baking sheets.

2. Sift together the flour, ginger, and baking soda into a bowl. Add the butter and rub into the flour until the mixture resembles fine bread crumbs, then stir in the brown sugar.

3. In another bowl, beat together the egg and corn syrup with a fork. Pour this mixture into the flour mixture and mix to make a smooth dough, kneading lightly with your hands.

4. Roll the dough out on a lightly floured surface to about ¼ inch thick and cut into shapes, using a star-shape cutter. Transfer the cookies to the prepared baking sheets.

5. Bake in the preheated oven for 10 minutes, or until golden brown. Remove the cookies from the oven and let cool for 5 minutes before transferring, using a spatula, to a wire rack to cool completely.

6. Once the cookies are cool, mix together the confectioners' sugar and lemon juice until smooth and place into a pastry bag fitted with a small tip. Pipe snowflake shapes onto each cookie, using the icing. Let set for a few hours.

2

4

6

Biscotti

 MAKES 30

 PREP TIME:
25 minutes
plus chilling

COOKING TIME:
10 minutes

nutritional information per cookie	125 cal, 8g fat, 4g sat fat, 5g total sugars, 0.15g salt

These classic Italian cookies have a wonderful crunchy texture—just right for dipping into a hot cappuccino coffee!

INGREDIENTS

2 sticks salted butter, softened
⅔ cup superfine sugar
finely grated rind of 1 lemon
1 egg yolk, lightly beaten
2 teaspoons brandy
2¼ cups all-purpose flour
pinch of salt
⅔ cup pistachio nuts
confectioners' sugar, for dusting

1. Put the butter, superfine sugar, and lemon rind into a bowl and mix well with a wooden spoon, then beat in the egg yolk and brandy. Sift together the flour and salt into the mixture and stir in the pistachio nuts until thoroughly combined.

2. Shape the mixture into a log, flatten slightly, wrap in plastic wrap, and chill in the refrigerator for 30–60 minutes.

3. Preheat the oven to 375°F. Line two baking sheets with parchment paper. Unwrap the log and cut it slightly on the diagonal into ¼-inch slices with a sharp, serrated knife. Put them on the prepared baking sheets, spaced well apart.

4. Bake in the preheated oven for 10 minutes, or until golden brown. Let cool on the baking sheets for 5–10 minutes, then, using a spatula, carefully transfer to wire racks to cool completely. Dust with confectioners' sugar.

1

2

3

SOMETHING DIFFERENT
Instead of the lemon and pistachios, try flavoring with orange rind and chopped blanched almonds.

Chocolate Chunk Shortbread

 MAKES 22

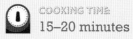 PREP TIME:
25 minutes
plus chilling

 COOKING TIME:
15–20 minutes

nutritional information
per cookie | 174 cal, 10g fat, 6g sat fat, 8.5g total sugars, 0.2g salt

Make classic shortbread even better by adding loads of delicious chocolate chunks!

INGREDIENTS

1¾ cups all-purpose flour

⅔ cup cornstarch, plus extra for dusting

4 ounces milk chocolate or semisweet chocolate

2 sticks salted butter, softened, plus extra for greasing

½ cup superfine sugar

1. Preheat the oven to 350°F. Lightly grease two baking sheets. Sift together the flour and cornstarch and set aside. Use a sharp knife to chop the chocolate into small chunks.

2. Put the butter and sugar into a bowl and beat with a wooden spoon until pale and creamy. Gradually stir in the flour and cornstarch and three-quarters of the chocolate chunks and mix to a soft dough. Halve the dough, shape into balls, and wrap in plastic wrap. Chill in the refrigerator for 20–25 minutes.

3. Lightly dust a surface with a little cornstarch and gently roll out the dough to a thickness of ½ inch. Using a 2¼-inch round cutter, stamp out 22 circles, rerolling the dough as necessary. Place the circles on the prepared baking sheets and top with the remaining chocolate chunks, pressing down lightly. Bake in the preheated oven for 15–20 minutes, or until just pale golden. Let cool on the baking sheets for 10 minutes, then transfer to a wire rack to cool completely.

Dark Chocolate & Nut Cookies

 MAKES 18   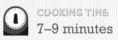 PREP TIME: 25 minutes plus cooling    COOKING TIME: 7–9 minutes

nutritional information **per cookie** | 197 cal, 12g fat, 5g sat fat, 11g total sugars, 0.1g salt

These crunchy nut cookies are dipped in melted chocolate to make them extra special.

INGREDIENTS

1⅔ cups all-purpose flour, plus extra for dusting

½ teaspoon baking soda

1 stick unsalted butter, chilled and diced, plus extra for greasing

⅓ cup firmly packed light brown sugar

2 tablespoons corn syrup

1 egg, beaten

⅓ cup blanched hazelnuts, chopped

½ cup chopped pecans

5 ouces semisweet chocolate, broken into pieces

1. Preheat the oven to 375°F. Lightly grease two large baking sheets.

2. Sift the flour and baking soda into a large bowl. Add the butter and rub it in with your fingertips until the mixture resembles fine bread crumbs. Stir in the sugar, syrup, egg, and two-thirds of the hazelnuts and pecans and mix thoroughly.

3. Drop tablespoonfuls of the dough onto the prepared baking sheets, spaced well apart. Flatten slightly with the back of the spoon and top with the remaining nuts.

4. Bake in the preheated oven for 7–9 minutes, or until golden brown. Let cool on the baking sheets for 5 minutes, then transfer to a wire rack to cool completely.

5. Melt the chocolate in a heatproof bowl set over a saucepan of simmering water. Dip the top of each cooled cookie in the chocolate, then let stand on a wire rack in a cool place until the chocolate has set.

2

3
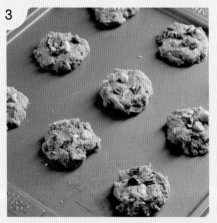

5

FREEZING TIP
The cookies will freeze
for up to two months,
interleaved with wax
paper in a freezer-
proof container. Thaw
at room temperature
for 1-2 hours.

Peanut Butter Cookies

 MAKES 15

 PREP TIME:
30 minutes
plus chilling

 COOKING TIME:
15 minutes

nutritional information per cookie	260 cal, 15g fat, 6g sat fat, 16g total sugars, 0.5g salt

Rich and buttery with a lovely peanut flavor, these simple cookies taste great with a glass of cold milk.

INGREDIENTS

1⅓ cups all-purpose flour

½ teaspoon baking powder

½ teaspoon salt

1 cup smooth peanut butter

1 stick salted butter, softened

1¼ teaspoons vanilla extract

½ cup firmly packed light brown sugar

½ cup superfine sugar

2 eggs

1. Sift together the flour, baking powder, and salt into a bowl and set aside. Beat together the peanut butter, butter, and vanilla extract until smooth in another bowl. Beat in the brown sugar and superfine sugar for 1 minute, then beat in the eggs one at a time. Stir in the flour mixture in two batches.

2. Halve the dough, shape into balls, wrap in plastic wrap, and chill in the refrigerator for at least 2 hours. Meanwhile, preheat the oven to 350°F. Line two baking sheets with parchment paper or leave uncovered and ungreased.

3. Roll or scoop the dough into 1½-inch balls and place them on the prepared baking sheets, spaced well apart. Use a fork to flatten each ball by making a crisscross pattern. Bake in the preheated oven for 15 minutes, or until golden. Remove the cookies from the oven and let cool on the baking sheet for 5 minutes. Using a spatula, transfer to a wire rack to cool completely.

1

2
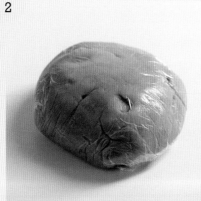

3

BE PREPARED
The wrapped cookie dough can be kept in the refrigerator for 2-3 days before baking.

Cookie Pops

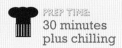 PREP TIME:
30 minutes
plus chilling

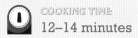 COOKING TIME:
12–14 minutes

nutritional information
per cookie | 115 cal, 5g fat, 3g sat fat, 9g total sugars, 0.2g salt

Perfect for parties, children will love these easy-to-eat chewy cookies on lollipop sticks.

INGREDIENTS

1 stick salted butter, softened, plus extra for greasing

½ cup firmly packed light brown sugar

½ cup superfine sugar

1 egg, lightly beaten

½ teaspoon vanilla extract

2 cups all-purpose flour

3 teaspoons baking powder

pinch of salt

24 lollipop sticks

2–3 tablespoons mini candy-coated chocolates

1. Preheat the oven to 350°F. Lightly grease three large baking sheets.

2. Place the butter and sugars in a bowl and beat together until pale and creamy, then gradually beat in the egg and vanilla extract. Sift together the flour, baking powder, and salt and stir into the mixture to make a soft dough. Knead lightly until smooth, then halve the dough, shape into balls, wrap in plastic wrap, and chill in the refrigerator for 30 minutes.

3. Divide the dough into 24 even pieces and roll each piece into a ball. Place on the prepared baking sheets, spaced well apart. Push a lollipop stick into each ball of dough at a slight angle. Lightly flatten each dough ball with your fingertips and top with 4–5 chocolates.

4. Bake in the preheated oven for 12–14 minutes, or until light golden. Let cool on the baking sheets for about 5 minutes, then carefully transfer to a wire rack to cool completely.

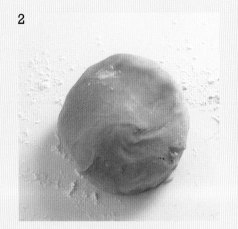

2

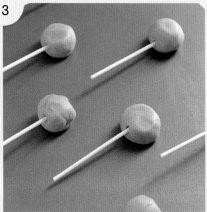

3

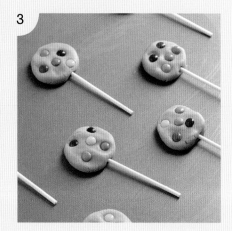

3

SOMETHING DIFFERENT

For double chocolate cookies, replace 3 tablespoons of the flour with unsweetened cocoa powder and top the cookies with milk chocolate or white chocolate chips.

Blueberry Cheesecake *218*

Caramel Pecan Cheesecake *220*

Lemon Cheesecake *222*

New York Cheesecake *224*

Cherry Cheesecake *226*

Caramel Popcorn *228*

Cappuccino Soufflés *230*

Date Cake with Caramel Sauce *232*

Molten Chocolate Lava Cakes *234*

Bread Pudding *236*

Coffee & Walnut Sponge Cakes *238*

Banana Pudding *240*

Baked Alaskas *242*

Baked Plums with Port *244*

Indian Pudding *246*

Apple & Blackberry Crisp *248*

Peach Cobbler *250*

Caramel Chocolate Puffs *252*

Brownie Sundae *254*

Tropical Rice Pudding *256*

Apple Turnovers *258*

Cinnamon Swirls *260*

Cream Puffs with Chocolate Sauce *262*

Baked Apples *264*

Desserts

Blueberry Cheesecake

 SERVES 10    PREP TIME: 1 hour plus chilling    COOKING TIME: 30 minutes

nutritional information per serving	550 cal, 42g fat, 24g sat fat, 26g total sugars, 0.8g salt

This cheesecake has a wonderfully smooth texture and is topped with plump blueberries in a sweet syrup.

INGREDIENTS

sunflower oil, for brushing
6 tablespoons salted butter
1¾ cups finely crushed Graham crackers
1¾ cups cream cheese
2 extra-large eggs
⅔ cup superfine sugar
1½ teaspoons vanilla extract
2 cups sour cream

topping
¼ cup superfine sugar
¼ cup water
1¾ cups fresh blueberries
1 teaspoon arrowroot

1. Preheat the oven to 375°F. Brush an 8-inch round springform cake pan with oil.

2. Melt the butter in a saucepan over low heat. Stir in the cookies, then press into the bottom of the prepared pan.

3. Place the cream cheese, eggs, ½ cup of the sugar, and ½ teaspoon of the vanilla extract in a food processor. Process until smooth. Pour over the cookie crust and smooth the top. Place on a baking sheet and bake in the preheated oven for 20 minutes, or until set. Remove from the oven and let cool for 20 minutes. Keep the oven turned on.

4. Mix the sour cream with the remaining sugar and vanilla extract in a bowl. Spoon over the cheesecake. Return it to the oven for 10 minutes, let cool, then cover with plastic wrap and chill in the refrigerator for 8 hours, or overnight.

5. To make the topping, place the sugar in a saucepan with 2 tablespoons of the water over low heat and stir until the sugar has dissolved. Increase the heat, add the blueberries, cover, and cook for a few minutes, or until they begin to soften. Remove from the heat. Mix the arrowroot and remaining water in a bowl, add to the blueberries, and stir until smooth. Return to low heat. Cook until the juice thickens and turns translucent. Let cool. Remove the cheesecake from the pan 1 hour before serving. Spoon over the blueberry topping and chill until ready to serve.

Caramel Pecan Cheesecake

 SERVES 12    PREP TIME: 40 minutes plus chilling    COOKING TIME: 45–50 minutes

nutritional information per serving	515 cal, 42g fat, 23g sat fat, 17g total sugars, 0.87g salt

This rich and indulgent baked cheesecake is perfect for a special occasion.

INGREDIENTS

2 cups finely crushed Graham crackers

3 tablespoons finely chopped pecans

6 tablespoons salted butter, melted, plus extra for greasing

2½ cups cream cheese

2 tablespoons light brown sugar

½ cup superfine sugar

3 extra-large eggs, beaten

1 teaspoon vanilla extract

1¼ cups sour cream

2 tablespoons cornstarch

topping

¼ cup dulce du leche (caramel sauce)

¼ cup chopped pecans

1. Preheat the oven to 325°F. Lightly grease a 9-inch round springform cake pan.

2. Put the crushed cookies and the nuts into a bowl and stir in the butter. Press into the bottom of the prepared cake pan. Chill in the refrigerator while making the filling.

3. Put the cheese and sugars into a large bowl and beat together until creamy. Gradually beat in the eggs and vanilla extract, then fold in the sour cream and cornstarch. Pour over the cookie crust.

4. Place on a baking sheet and bake in the preheated oven for 45–50 minutes, or until just set (the middle should still wobble slightly). Turn off the heat, open the oven door, and let the cheesecake stand in the oven until cold. Chill in the refrigerator for 3–4 hours or overnight.

5. Unclip the pan and transfer the cheesecake to a serving plate. To make the topping, gently spread the dulce du leche over the top of the cheesecake and sprinkle with the nuts.

Lemon Cheesecake

 SERVES 8    PREP TIME: 30 minutes plus chilling   COOKING TIME: 40–45 minutes

nutritional information
per serving   338 cal, 19g fat, 10g sat fat, 22g total sugars, 0.55g salt

With a gingersnap crust and creamy lemon filling, this cheesecake makes a refreshing summer dessert.

INGREDIENTS

4 tablespoons salted butter, plus extra for greasing
1½ cups crushed gingersnaps
3 lemons
1¼ cups ricotta cheese
1 cup Greek-style yogurt
4 eggs, beaten
1 tablespoon cornstarch
½ cup superfine sugar
strips of lemon zest, to decorate
confectioners' sugar, for dusting

1. Preheat the oven to 350°F. Grease an 8-inch round springform cake pan and line with parchment paper.

2. Melt the butter in a saucepan and stir in the cookie crumbs. Press into the bottom of the prepared cake pan. Chill until firm.

3. Meanwhile, finely grate the rind from the lemons into a bowl and squeeze the juice. Add the ricotta, yogurt, eggs, cornstarch, and superfine sugar and beat until a smooth batter is formed.

4. Carefully spoon the batter into the pan. Bake in the preheated oven for 40–45 minutes, or until just firm and golden brown.

5. Cool the cheesecake completely in the pan, then run a knife around the edge to loosen and turn out onto a serving plate. Decorate with lemon zest and dust with confectioners' sugar.

2

3

4

GOES WELL WITH *Serve with a spoonful of crème fraîche or Greek-style yogurt.*

New York Cheesecake

 SERVES 10    PREP TIME: 40 minutes plus chilling    COOKING TIME: 55 minutes

nutritional information per serving	845 cal, 73g fat, 44g sat fat, 29g total sugars, 1.1g salt

This traditional cheesecake from the Big Apple has a sweet cookie crust and rich vanilla- and citrus-flavor filling.

INGREDIENTS

1 stick salted butter, plus extra for greasing

1¼ cups finely crushed Graham crackers

1 tablespoon granulated sugar

4 cups cream cheese

1¼ cups superfine sugar

2 tablespoons all-purpose flour

1 teaspoon vanilla extract

finely grated zest of 1 orange

finely grated zest of 1 lemon

3 eggs

2 egg yolks

1¼ cups heavy cream

1. Preheat the oven to 350°F. Melt the butter in a small saucepan. Remove from the heat and stir in the cookies and sugar. Press the cookie mixture tightly into the bottom of a 9-inch round springform cake pan. Place in the preheated oven and bake for 10 minutes. Remove from the oven and let cool on a wire rack.

2. Increase the oven temperature to 400°F. Use an electric mixer to beat the cheese until creamy, then gradually add the superfine sugar and flour and beat until smooth. Increase the speed and beat in the vanilla extract, orange zest, and lemon zest, then beat in the eggs and egg yolks one at a time. Finally, beat in the cream. Scrape any excess from the sides and beaters of the mixture into the mixture. It should be light and fluffy—beat on a faster setting if you need to.

3. Grease the sides of the cake pan and pour in the filling. Smooth the top, transfer to the oven, and bake for 15 minutes, then reduce the temperature to 225°F and bake for an additional 30 minutes. Turn off the oven and let the cheesecake stand in it for 2 hours to cool and set. Chill in the refrigerator overnight before serving.

4. Slide a knife around the edge of the cake, then unclip and remove from the pan to serve.

1

1

3

Cherry Cheesecake

 SERVES 8    PREP TIME: 40 minutes plus chilling   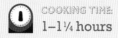 COOKING TIME: 1–1¼ hours

nutritional information per serving	554 cal, 35g fat, 17g sat fat, 44g total sugars, 0.7g salt

Ricotta cheese and Greek-style yogurt give this cheesecake a tangy flavor, which is perfectly complemented by the sweet cherry topping.

INGREDIENTS

1½ cups finely crushed shortbread cookies

5 tablespoons salted butter, melted, plus extra for greasing

1 cup ricotta cheese

1 cup cream cheese

⅔ cup superfine sugar

finely grated rind and juice of 1 small lemon

3 eggs, beaten

1¼ cups Greek-style yogurt

1 tablespoon cornstarch

topping

2 cups pitted fresh cherries

¼ cup superfine sugar

⅓ cup water

1 tablespoon arrowroot

1. Preheat the oven to 300°F. Lightly grease an 8-inch round springform cake pan.

2. Put the crushed cookies into a bowl and stir in the butter. Press the cookie mixture tightly into the bottom of the prepared cake pan. Chill in the refrigerator while making the filling.

3. Put the ricotta cheese, cream cheese, and sugar into a large bowl and beat together until creamy. Stir in the lemon rind and juice, then gradually beat in the eggs. Fold in the yogurt and cornstarch and pour the filling over the cookie crust.

4. Place on a baking sheet and bake in the preheated oven for 1–1¼ hours, or until just set (the middle should still wobble slightly). Turn off the heat, open the oven door, and let the cheesecake stand in the oven until cold. Chill in the refrigerator for 3–4 hours or overnight.

5. To make the topping, put the cherries and sugar into a saucepan with ¼ cup of the water and heat gently until the sugar dissolves. Simmer for 5 minutes. Blend the arrowroot to a thin paste with the remaining water and stir into the cherries. Simmer for an additional 2–3 minutes, stirring continuously, or until the syrup has thickened. Let cool.

6. To serve, unclip the cheesecake and transfer to a serving plate. Top with the cherries and syrup.

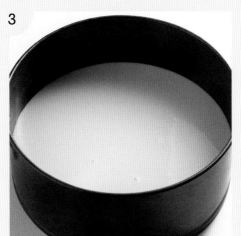

Caramel Popcorn

 SERVES 4    PREP TIME: 20 minutes    COOKING TIME: 10 minutes

nutritional information per serving	484 cal, 30g fat, 14g sat fat, 41g total sugars, 0.4g salt

Turn popcorn into a sweet snack by coating in caramel and drizzling with chocolate!

INGREDIENTS

1 tablespoon sunflower oil, plus extra for greasing

½ cup popping corn

6 tablespoons salted butter

½ cup firmly packed light brown sugar

2 tablespoons corn syrup

¼ cup chopped pecans

2 ounces milk chocolate, melted

1. Preheat the oven to 325°F. Lightly grease a large baking sheet.

2. Heat the oil in a large saucepan. Add the popping corn, cover, and cook over high heat for 3–4 minutes, shaking occasionally, until all the popcorn has popped.

3. Place the butter, sugar, and syrup in a saucepan and heat gently until the butter has melted. Bring to a boil and let the mixture bubble rapidly for 1 minute. Quickly pour the hot caramel over the warm popcorn, add the chopped pecans, and mix thoroughly.

4. Spread the popcorn over the baking sheet and bake in the preheated oven for 10 minutes. Let cool, then break into smaller pieces.

5. Drizzle the melted chocolate over the caramel popcorn and let stand until set. Serve in small bowls, paper cones, or cupcake liners.

2

3

4

BE PREPARED
You can make
this caramel
popcorn the day
before serving.
Store in an
airtight container.

Cappuccino Soufflés

🍽 SERVES 6   👨‍🍳 PREP TIME: 20 minutes   ⏲ COOKING TIME: 15 minutes

nutritional information per serving	282 cal, 18g fat, 10g sat fat, 22g total sugars, 0.2g salt

These individual hot chocolate and coffee soufflés are really simple to make but look very impressive.

INGREDIENTS

⅓ cup heavy whipping cream

2 teaspoons instant espresso coffee granules

2 tablespoons Kahlúa

butter, for greasing

3 extra-large eggs, separated, plus 1 extra egg white

2 tablespoons superfine sugar, plus extra for coating

5 ounces semisweet chocolate, melted and cooled

unsweetened cocoa powder, for dusting

1. Place the cream in a small, heavy saucepan and heat gently. Stir in the coffee until it has dissolved, then stir in the Kahlúa. Divide the coffee mixture among six lightly greased ¾-cup ramekins (individual ceramic dishes) coated with superfine sugar. Preheat the oven to 375°F.

2. Place the egg whites in a clean, grease-free bowl and beat until soft peaks form, then gradually beat in the sugar until stiff but not dry. Stir together the egg yolks and melted chocolate in a separate bowl, then stir in a little of the beatened egg whites. Gradually fold in the remaining egg whites.

3. Divide the mixture among the prepared ramekins. Place the ramekins on a baking sheet and bake in the preheated oven for 15 minutes, or until just set. Dust with sifted cocoa powder and serve immediately.

1

2

3

COOK'S NOTE
For a well-risen soufflé, make sure the oven is preheated to the correct temperature.

Date Cake
with Caramel Sauce

 SERVES 4    PREP TIME: 30 minutes   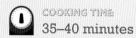 COOKING TIME: 35–40 minutes

nutritional information per serving	1,007 cal, 41g fat, 24g sat fat, 121g total sugars, 1.8g salt

A moist and fruity date and golden raisin cake, smothered in a smooth, warm caramel sauce—serve with whipped cream for dessert heaven!

INGREDIENTS

½ cup golden raisins

1 cup chopped, pitted dates

1 teaspoon baking soda

2 tablespoons butter, softened, plus extra for greasing

1 cup firmly packed light brown sugar

2 eggs, beaten

1⅔ cups all-purpose flour

2¼ teaspoons baking powder

zested rind of 1 orange, to decorate

freshly whipped cream, to serve (optional)

sauce

2 tablespoons butter

¾ cup heavy cream

1 cup firmly packed light brown sugar

1. To make the sponge, put the golden raisins, dates, and baking soda into a heatproof bowl. Cover with boiling water and let soak for 10 minutes.

2. Preheat the oven to 350°F. Grease an 8-inch round cake pan.

3. Put the butter in a separate bowl, add the sugar, and beat together until creamy. Gradually beat in the eggs. Sift in the flour and baking powder, then fold into the mixture. Drain the soaked fruit, add to the bowl, and mix. Spoon the batter evenly into the prepared cake pan.

4. Transfer to the preheated oven and bake for 35–40 minutes. The sponge is cooked when a toothpick inserted into the center comes out clean.

5. About 5 minutes before the end of the cooking time, make the sauce. Melt the butter in a saucepan over medium heat. Stir in the cream and sugar and bring to a boil, stirring continuously. Reduce the heat and simmer for 5 minutes.

6. Turn out the dessert onto a serving plate and pour the sauce over the top. Decorate with zested orange rind and serve with whipped cream, if using.

1

3

5

Molten Chocolate Lava Cakes

 SERVES 4    PREP TIME: 20 minutes   COOKING TIME: 12–15 minutes

nutritional information per serving	502 cal, 33g fat, 19g sat fat, 41g total sugars, 0.5g salt

Everyone will love these divine desserts with their hidden centers of molten chocolate.

INGREDIENTS

1 stick salted butter, plus extra for greasing

4 ounces semisweet chocolate, broken into pieces

2 extra-large eggs, beaten

1 teaspoon vanilla extract

½ cup superfine sugar, plus extra for sprinkling

2 tablespoons all-purpose flour

confectioners' sugar, for dusting

heavy cream, to serve (optional)

1. Preheat the oven to 400°F. Grease four ¾-cup ramekins (individual ceramic dishes) and sprinkle with superfine sugar.

2. Place the butter and chocolate in a heatproof bowl set over a saucepan of simmering water and heat until melted. Stir until smooth. Set aside.

3. Place the eggs, vanilla extract, superfine sugar, and flour in a bowl and beat together. Stir in the melted chocolate mixture. Pour into the prepared ramekins and place on a baking sheet. Bake in the preheated oven for 12–15 minutes, or until the desserts are well risen and set on the outside but still molten inside.

4. Let stand for 1 minute, then invert the desserts onto serving plates. Dust with confectioners' sugar and serve immediately with the cream, if using.

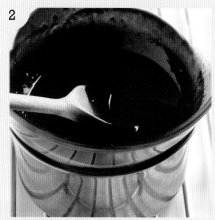

Bread Pudding

 SERVES 8

 PREP TIME:
30 minutes
plus chilling

 COOKING TIME:
1½ hours

nutritional information
per serving
949 cal, 34g fat, 20g sat fat, 114g total sugars, 1.8g salt

This warming pudding is a great way to use up stale bread and mixed dried fruit.

INGREDIENTS

2½ cups whole milk

1 stick salted butter, diced, plus extra for greasing

1 tablespoon allspice

¼ teaspoon ground cloves

½ teaspoon ground nutmeg

18 slices day-old white bread, torn into pieces

1⅔ cups firmly packed light brown sugar, plus 2 tablespoons extra for sprinkling

3 cups mixed dried fruit, such as raisins, golden raisins, and currants

¼ cup finely chopped dried apricots

2 extra-large eggs, beaten

finely grated zest of ½ lemon

rum sauce

1 cup confectioners' sugar

⅓ cup firmly packed light brown sugar

1¼ sticks salted butter, softened

4 teaspoons whole milk

2 tablespoons light or dark rum

finely grated zest of ½ lemon

1. To make the sauce, sift the confectioners' sugar and brown sugar into a small bowl and set aside. Beat the butter in another bowl until it is soft and creamy. Gradually beat the sugars into the butter, alternating with the milk and rum. Stir in the lemon zest, being careful not to overbeat or the mixture will separate. Transfer the sauce to a serving bowl, cover, and chill for at least 30 minutes, until firm.

2. Put the milk, butter, and spices into a large saucepan over medium heat and heat until small bubbles appear. Add the bread, brown sugar, mixed dried fruit, and apricots and stir together until well blended and the bread starts to break down. Remove from the heat and let stand for 20 minutes.

3. Meanwhile, preheat the oven to 350°F and grease an 8-inch square baking dish. Stir the pudding mixture again to distribute the fruit evenly. Stir in the eggs and lemon zest. Spoon the mixture into the prepared dish, smooth the surface, and sprinkle with brown sugar.

4. Bake in the preheated oven for 1½ hours, or until it is set and crusty on top. Cut into pieces and serve immediately with the sauce.

Coffee & Walnut Sponge Cakes

 SERVES 6  PREP TIME: 35 minutes  COOKING TIME: 30–40 minutes

nutritional information per serving	410 cal, 27g fat, 11g sat fat, 18g total sugars, 0.6g salt

These sponges are light and fluffy, and are perfect with the sweet, nutty butterscotch sauce.

INGREDIENTS

1 tablespoon instant coffee powder

1¼ cups all-purpose flour

1¾ teaspoons baking powder

1 teaspoon ground cinnamon

4 tablespoons salted butter, softened, plus extra for greasing

¼ cup firmly packed light brown sugar

2 extra-large eggs, beaten

½ cup finely chopped walnuts

butterscotch sauce

¼ cup coarsely chopped walnuts

4 tablespoons salted butter

¼ cup firmly packed light brown sugar

1. Dissolve the coffee powder in 2 tablespoons of boiling water and set aside. Sift the flour, baking powder, and cinnamon into a bowl. Place the butter and sugar in a separate bowl and beat together until creamy. Gradually beat in the eggs. Add a little of the flour mixture if it shows signs of curdling. Fold in half the flour-and-cinnamon mixture, then fold in the remaining flour-and-cinnamon mixture, alternately with the coffee and walnuts. Preheat the oven to 375°F.

2. Divide the batter evenly among six greased individual molds. Place a piece of greased aluminum foil over each mold and secure with a rubber band. Stand the molds in a baking pan and pour in enough boiling water to reach halfway up the sides of the molds. Cover the baking pan with a tent of foil, folding it under the rim.

3. Bake in the preheated oven for 30–40 minutes, or until well risen and firm to the touch. Meanwhile, make the sauce. Place all the ingredients in a saucepan over low heat and stir until melted and blended. Bring to a simmer, then remove from the heat. Invert the cakes onto a serving plate, spoon the hot sauce over them, and serve.

1

2

3

FREEZING TIP
Freeze for up
to two months.
Thaw for
3-4 hours at
room temperature,
then reheat.

Banana Pudding

 SERVES 4    PREP TIME: 25 minutes plus chilling    COOKING TIME: 4–5 minutes

nutritional information per serving	852 cal, 71g fat, 44g sat fat, 39g total sugars, 0.4g salt

Buttery light cookies, vanilla cream, and sliced bananas all combine to make this fabulous layered dessert.

INGREDIENTS

3 tablespoons salted butter, softened, plus extra for greasing

3 tablespoons superfine sugar

1 egg white, lightly beaten

⅓ cup all-purpose flour

½ teaspoon baking powder

2 cups heavy cream

1 teaspoon vanilla extract

⅔ cup prepared vanilla pudding

2 bananas

2 teaspoons lemon juice

2 tablespoons demerara sugar or other raw sugar

1. Preheat the oven to 425°F. Grease two large baking sheets.

2. Put the butter and superfine sugar into a bowl and beat until pale and creamy. Gradually beat in the egg white. Sift in the flour and baking powder, then fold in. Drop about 30 tiny spoonfuls of the dough onto the prepared baking sheets, spaced well apart.

3. Bake in the preheated oven for 4–5 minutes, or until deep golden brown around the edges. Loosen the cookies from the baking sheets with a spatula, transfer to a wire rack, and let cool completely. Put the cream into a bowl with the vanilla extract and whip until it holds firm peaks. Fold in the vanilla pudding. Thinly slice the bananas and toss them in the lemon juice.

4. To assemble the desserts, layer almost all the cookies with the vanilla cream and bananas in four individual serving glasses. Crush the remaining cookies, mix with the demerara sugar, and sprinkle over the top of the desserts. Chill for 1 hour before serving.

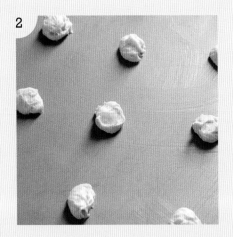
2

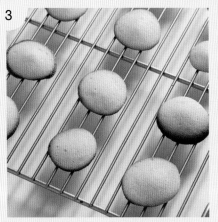
3

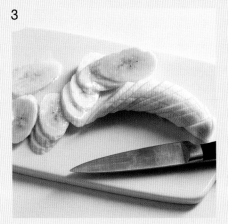
3

Baked Alaskas

 SERVES 4    PREP TIME: 20 minutes plus freezing   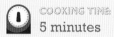 COOKING TIME: 5 minutes

nutritional information per serving	634 cal, 23g fat, 7g sat fat, 82g total sugars, 0.7g salt

These spectacular hot desserts are easy to prepare ahead and take just minutes to cook.

INGREDIENTS

¼ cup raisins or golden raisins

3 tablespoons dark rum or ginger wine

4 square slices ginger cake

4 scoops vanilla ice cream or rum and raisin ice cream

3 egg whites

1 cup granulated sugar or superfine sugar

1. Preheat the oven to 450°F. Mix the raisins with the rum in a small bowl.

2. Place the cake slices, spaced well apart, on a baking sheet and scatter a tablespoonful of the soaked raisins on each slice.

3. Place a scoop of ice cream in the center of each slice and place in the freezer.

4. Meanwhile, beat the egg whites in a clean, grease-free bowl until soft peaks form. Gradually beat the sugar into the egg whites, a tablespoonful at a time, until the mixture forms stiff peaks.

5. Remove the ice cream-topped cake slices from the freezer and spoon the meringue over the ice cream. Spread to cover the ice cream completely.

6. Bake in the preheated oven for about 5 minutes, or until starting to brown. Serve immediately.

Baked Plums with Port

 SERVES 4    PREP TIME: 25 minutes    COOKING TIME: 30–40 minutes

nutritional information per serving	161 cal, 0g fat, 0g sat fat, 26g total sugars, trace salt

Fresh and juicy plums gently baked in a sweet, spiced port syrup—such a simple dessert but so delicious!

INGREDIENTS

8 large plums
1 cinnamon stick
2 strips pared orange rind
2 tablespoons light brown sugar
2 tablespoons honey
1 cup port
thick cream or Greek-style yogurt, to serve (optional)

1. Preheat the oven to 350°F. Halve and pit the plums.

2. Place the plum halves cut side up in a small ovenproof baking dish with the cinnamon stick and orange rind. Sprinkle with the sugar. Mix together the honey and port and pour around the plums.

3. Bake in the preheated oven for 30–40 minutes, or until the plums are soft. Let cool for 5 minutes, then pour off the liquid into a small saucepan.

4. Bring the liquid to a boil, then simmer for 5–10 minutes, or until syrupy and reduced by about one-third. Pour the syrup over the plums. Serve warm or cold with cream, if using.

1

2

2

Indian Pudding

 SERVES 6    PREP TIME: 35 minutes   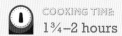 COOKING TIME: 1¾–2 hours

nutritional information per serving	213 cal, 10g fat, 5g sat fat, 16.5g total sugars, 0.5g salt

This dessert from New England is made with cornmeal and has a wonderful sweet and spicy flavor.

INGREDIENTS

2 tablespoons raisins

⅓ cup cornmeal

1½ cups whole milk

¼ cup dark molasses

2 tablespoons dark brown sugar

½ teaspoon salt

2 tablespoons salted butter, diced, plus extra for greasing

2 teaspoons ground ginger

¼ teaspoon cinnamon

¼ teaspoon ground nutmeg

2 eggs, beaten

vanilla ice cream, to serve

1. Preheat the oven to 300°F. Generously grease a 1-quart baking dish and set aside. Put the raisins in a strainer with 1 tablespoon of the cornmeal and toss well together. Shake off the excess cornmeal and set aside.

2. Put the milk and molasses into a saucepan over medium–high heat and stir until the molasses is dissolved. Add the sugar and salt and continue stirring until the sugar is dissolved. Sprinkle with the remaining cornmeal and bring to a boil, stirring continuously. Reduce the heat and simmer for 3–5 minutes, or until the mixture is thickened. Remove the pan from the heat, add the butter, ginger, cinnamon, and nutmeg, and stir until the butter is melted. Add the eggs and beat until they are incorporated, then stir in the raisins. Pour the mixture into the prepared dish.

3. Put the dish in a small baking pan and pour in enough boiling water to come halfway up the side of the dish. Put the dish in the preheated oven and bake, uncovered, for 1¾–2 hours, or until set and a toothpick inserted in the center comes out clean. Serve with ice cream.

1

2

3

GOES WELL WITH
Try serving with
thick yogurt
sweetened with
honey instead
of the ice cream.

Apple & Blackberry Crisp

 SERVES 4   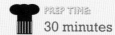 PREP TIME: 30 minutes   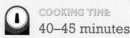 COOKING TIME: 40–45 minutes

nutritional information per serving	554 cal, 25g fat, 16g sat fat, 49g total sugars, 0.2g salt

Tart apples and blackberries with a sugary, sweet crumb topping—it's the ultimate winter warmer!

INGREDIENTS

5 cooking apples, such as Granny Smith or Pippin (about 2 pounds)

2 cups blackberries, fresh or frozen

¼ cup firmly packed light brown sugar

1 teaspoon ground cinnamon

ice cream or cream, to serve (optional)

crumb topping

⅔ cup all-purpose flour

1 teaspoon baking powder

⅔ cup whole-wheat flour

1 stick unsalted butter, diced

¼ cup demerara sugar or other raw sugar

1. Preheat the oven to 400°F. Peel and core the apples, then cut them into chunks. Put them in a bowl with the blackberries, brown sugar, and cinnamon and mix together, then transfer to a 1-quart baking dish.

2. To make the crumb topping, sift the all-purpose flour and baking powder into a bowl and stir in the whole-wheat flour. Rub in the butter with your fingertips until the mixture resembles coarse bread crumbs. Stir in the demerara sugar.

3. Spread the crumb topping over the fruit and bake in the preheated oven for 40–45 minutes, or until the apples are soft and the crumb is golden brown and crisp. Serve with ice cream or cream, if using.

1

2

3

BE PREPARED
Make up a double batch of the crumb topping and freeze for another day.

Peach Cobbler

 SERVES 6    PREP TIME: 25 minutes    COOKING TIME: 35 minutes

nutritional information
per serving   390 cal, 14g fat, 8g sat fat, 38g total sugars, 0.9g salt

This traditional fruit cobbler has a crumbly biscuit topping that is baked until crisp and golden.

INGREDIENTS

filling

6 peaches, peeled and sliced
¼ cup superfine sugar
½ tablespoon lemon juice
1½ teaspoons cornstarch
½ teaspoon almond extract
or vanilla extract
ice cream, to serve

topping

1½ cups all-purpose flour
½ cup superfine sugar
1½ teaspoons baking powder
½ teaspoon salt
6 tablespoons salted butter, diced
1 egg
⅓ cup plus 1 tablespoon milk

1. Preheat the oven to 425°F. Place the peaches in a 9-inch square baking dish. Add the sugar, lemon juice, cornstarch, and almond extract and toss together. Bake in the preheated oven for 20 minutes.

2. Meanwhile, to make the topping, sift the flour, all but 2 tablespoons of the sugar, the baking powder, and salt into a bowl. Rub in the butter with your fingertips until the mixture resembles bread crumbs. Mix the egg and ⅓ cup of the milk in a bowl, then mix the wet ingredients into the dry ingredients with a fork until a soft, sticky dough forms. If the dough seems too dry, stir in the extra tablespoon of milk.

3. Reduce the oven temperature to 400°F. Remove the peaches from the oven and drop spoonfuls of the topping over the surface, without smoothing. Sprinkle with the remaining sugar, return to the oven, and bake for an additional 15 minutes, or until the topping is golden brown and firm—the topping will spread as it cooks. Serve hot or at room temperature, with ice cream.

SOMETHING DIFFERENT *Instead of the peaches, try halved apricots or plums.*

Caramel Chocolate Puffs

 SERVES 6

 PREP TIME:
30 minutes
plus chilling

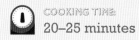 COOKING TIME:
20–25 minutes

nutritional information
per serving

707 cal, 52g fat, 29g sat fat, 30g total sugars, 0.6g salt

*Crisp and buttery puff pastry shells with a rich,
creamy chocolate and caramel filling.*

INGREDIENTS

1½ sheets ready-to-bake
puff pastry (about 14 ounces)

5 ounces semisweet chocolate,
broken into pieces

1¼ cups heavy cream

¼ cup superfine sugar

4 egg yolks

¼ cup store-bought
dulce de leche (caramel sauce)

whipped cream, to serve

unsweetened cocoa powder,
for dusting

1. Line the bottoms of a 12-cup muffin pan with circles of parchment paper. Cut out twelve 2-inch circles from an edge of the pastry and cut the remainder into 12 strips. Roll the strips to half their thickness and line the sides of each pan cup with a strip. Place a circle of pastry in the bottom of each cup and press together to seal, making a tart shell. Prick the bottoms with a fork and chill in the refrigerator for 30 minutes.

2. Preheat the oven to 400°F. While the pastry is chilling, place the chocolate in a heatproof bowl, set the bowl over a saucepan of gently simmering water, and heat until melted. Let cool slightly, then stir in the cream.

3. Place the sugar and egg yolks in a bowl and beat together, then mix well with the melted chocolate. Place a teaspoonful of the dulce de leche into each tart shell, then divide the chocolate mixture evenly among the tarts. Bake in the preheated oven for 20–25 minutes, turning the pan around halfway through cooking, until just set. Let cool in the pan, then remove carefully and serve with whipped cream, dusted with cocoa.

1
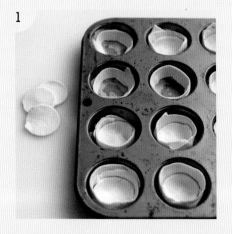

2

3

COOK'S NOTE
Put the muffin pan onto a preheated baking sheet to help cook the pastry bottoms.

Brownie Sundae

 SERVES 6    PREP TIME: 30 minutes plus cooling   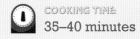 COOKING TIME: 35–40 minutes

nutritional information per serving	870 cal, 55g fat, 32g sat fat, 72g total sugars, 0.9g salt

This is a great dessert to serve for a crowd at a party or barbecue—simply cut up the brownies and let the guests help themselves to ice cream, chocolate sauce, nuts, and cherries.

INGREDIENTS

6 ounces semisweet chocolate, broken into pieces

1½ sticks salted butter, plus extra for greasing

¾ cup firmly packed light brown sugar

3 eggs, beaten

1 cup all-purpose flour

1½ teaspoons baking powder

chocolate fudge sauce

2 ounces semisweet chocolate, broken into pieces

¼ cup firmly packed light brown sugar

4 tablespoons unsalted butter

3 tablespoons milk

to serve

6 large scoops of vanilla ice cream

1 tablespoon chopped pecans

6 fresh or maraschino cherries

1. Preheat the oven to 350°F. Grease an 8-inch square cake pan and line with parchment paper.

2. For the brownies, place the chocolate and butter in a large heatproof bowl set over a saucepan of simmering water and heat until melted. Cool for 5 minutes, then beat in the sugar and eggs. Sift in the flour and baking powder and fold in. Pour the batter into the prepared cake pan and bake in the preheated oven for 35–40 minutes, or until risen and just firm to the touch. Let cool in the pan for 15 minutes, then invert onto a wire rack to cool completely.

3. For the sauce, place all the ingredients in a saucepan and heat gently, stirring all the time until melted. Bring to a boil and let simmer for 1 minute. Remove from the heat and let cool.

4. To serve, cut the brownies into six pieces. Place each piece on a serving plate and top with a large scoop of ice cream. Spoon over the warm sauce and decorate with chopped pecan nuts and cherries.

Tropical Rice Pudding

 SERVES 4    PREP TIME: 10 minutes   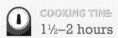 COOKING TIME: 1½–2 hours

nutritional information per serving	370 cal, 17g fat, 14g sat fat, 33g total sugars, 0.14g salt

Traditional rice pudding is given a complete makeover with tropical fruit and coconut milk.

INGREDIENTS

butter, for greasing

¼ cup short-grain rice

1 cup chopped dried tropical fruit, such as mango, papaya, and pineapple

2 tablespoons superfine sugar

1¼ cups coconut milk

1¼ cups whole milk

fresh or canned mango slices, to serve

strips of lime zest, to decorate

1. Preheat the oven to 300°F. Grease a shallow 1¼-quart baking dish.

2. Put the rice, dried fruit, and sugar into the prepared dish. Pour over the coconut milk and whole milk and stir well.

3. Place the dish on a baking sheet in the preheated oven and bake for 1½–2 hours, or until the rice is tender and most of the liquid has been absorbed. Stir thoroughly two or three times during baking to prevent a skin from forming.

4. Serve hot or cold in individual serving dishes with mango slices, decorated with strips of lime zest.

SOMETHING
DIFFERENT
Scoop the seeds and
pulp from two passion
fruit and stir into the
rice pudding when it
comes out of the oven.

Apple Turnovers

 MAKES 8 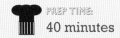 PREP TIME: 40 minutes 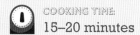 COOKING TIME: 15–20 minutes

nutritional information per pastry	326 cal, 24g fat, 14g sat fat, 14g total sugars, 0.3g salt

Quick and easy to make, these sweet pastries are a great way to use up a bumper crop of apples.

INGREDIENTS

1 sheet ready-to-bake puff pastry (9 ounces), thawed, if frozen

flour, for dusting

milk, for glazing

filling
2 large cooking apples (about 1 pound), such as Granny Smith or Pippin, peeled, cored, and chopped

grated rind of 1 lemon (optional)

pinch of ground cloves (optional)

3 tablespoons sugar

orange sugar
1 tablespoon sugar, for sprinkling

finely grated rind of 1 orange

orange cream
1 cup heavy cream

grated rind of 1 orange and juice of ½ orange

confectioners' sugar, to taste

1. To make the filling, mix together the apples, lemon rind, and ground cloves, if using, but do not add the sugar yet because the juice will seep out of the apples. For the orange sugar, mix together the sugar and orange rind.

2. Preheat the oven to 425°F. Roll out the pastry on a floured surface into a 24 x 12-inch rectangle. Cut the pastry in half lengthwise, then across into four to make eight 6-inch squares.

3. Mix the sugar into the apple filling. Brush each square lightly with milk and place a little of the apple filling in the center. Fold over one corner diagonally to meet the opposite one, making a triangular turnover, and press the edges together firmly. Place on a baking sheet. Repeat with the remaining squares. Brush with milk and sprinkle with the orange sugar. Bake in the preheated oven for 15–20 minutes, or until browned. Let cool on a wire rack.

4. For the orange cream, whip together the cream, orange rind, and orange juice until thick. Add a little confectioners' sugar to taste and whip again until it just holds soft peaks. Serve the turnovers warm with orange cream.

Cinnamon Swirls

 MAKES 12    PREP TIME: 1 hour plus rising   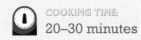 COOKING TIME: 20–30 minutes

nutritional information per pastry	170 cal, 8g fat, 5g sat fat, 9g total sugars, 0.3g salt

These homemade Danish pastries taste delicious warm, straight from the oven, for a mid morning treat.

INGREDIENTS

1⅔ cups white bread flour
½ teaspoon salt
2¼ teaspoons active dry yeast
2 tablespoons butter, cut into small pieces, plus extra for greasing
1 egg, lightly beaten
½ cup lukewarm milk
2 tablespoons maple syrup, for glazing

filling
4 tablespoons butter, softened
2 teaspoons ground cinnamon
¼ cup firmly packed light brown sugar
⅓ cup dried currants

1. Grease a baking sheet with a little butter.

2. Sift the flour and salt into a mixing bowl. Stir in the yeast. Rub in the butter with your fingertips until the mixture resembles bread crumbs. Add the egg and milk and mix to form a dough.

3. Form the dough into a ball, place in a greased bowl, cover with plastic wrap, and let stand in a warm place for about 40 minutes, or until doubled in size. Knead the dough for 1 minute, then roll out to a rectangle measuring 12 x 9 inches.

4. To make the filling, cream together the butter, cinnamon, and sugar until light and fluffy. Spread the filling evenly over the dough rectangle, leaving a 1-inch border all around. Sprinkle the currants evenly over the top.

5. Roll up the dough from one of the long edges, and press down to seal. Cut the roll into 12 slices. Place them on the baking sheet, cover, and let stand for 30 minutes.

6. Meanwhile, preheat the oven to 375°F. Bake the swirls in the preheated oven for 20–30 minutes, or until well risen. Brush with the maple syrup and let cool slightly before serving.

Cream Puffs
with Chocolate Sauce

 SERVES 4    PREP TIME: 40 minutes    COOKING TIME: 25 minutes

nutritional information per serving	948 cal, 77g fat, 46g sat fat, 32g total sugars, 0.2g salt

This classic dessert of crisp choux pastry buns filled with vanilla cream and drizzled with hot chocolate sauce never fails to impress.

INGREDIENTS

choux pastry dough
5 tablespoons unsalted butter, plus extra for greasing
¾ cup plus 2 tablespoons water
¾ cup plus 1 tablespoon all-purpose flour
3 eggs, beaten

cream filling
1¼ cups heavy cream
3 tablespoons superfine sugar
1 teaspoon vanilla extract

chocolate & brandy sauce
4 ounces semisweet chocolate, broken into small pieces
2 tablespoons unsalted butter
⅓ cup water
2 tablespoons brandy

1. Preheat the oven to 400°F. Grease several large baking sheets.

2. To make the dough, place the butter and water in a saucepan and bring to a boil. Meanwhile, sift the flour into a bowl. Turn off the heat and beat in the flour until smooth. Cool for 5 minutes. Beat in enough of the eggs to give the mixture a soft, dropping consistency.

3. Transfer to a pastry bag fitted with a ½-inch plain tip. Pipe small balls onto the prepared baking sheets. Bake in the preheated oven for 25 minutes. Remove from the oven. Pierce each ball with a toothpick to let the steam escape.

4. To make the filling, whip together the cream, sugar, and vanilla extract. Cut the pastry balls across the middle, then fill with cream.

5. To make the sauce, gently melt together the chocolate, butter, and water in a small saucepan, stirring continuously, until smooth. Stir in the brandy.

6. Pile the cream puffs into individual serving dishes, pour over the sauce, and serve.

Baked Apples

 SERVES 4    PREP TIME: 20 minutes    COOKING TIME: 40–45 minutes

nutritional information per serving	230 cal, 3g fat, 0.5g sat fat, 34g total sugars, trace salt

A fruity filling and a sweet red wine glaze give simple baked apples the star treatment.

INGREDIENTS

4 cooking apples, such as Granny Smith

1 tablespoon lemon juice

⅓ cup blueberries

⅓ cup raisins

¼ cup mixed nuts, chopped and toasted

½ teaspoon ground cinnamon

2 tablespoons light brown sugar

1 cup red wine

2 teaspoons cornstarch

4 teaspoons water

heavy cream, to serve (optional)

1. Preheat the oven to 400°F. Using a sharp knife, score a line around the center of each apple. Core the apples, then brush the centers with the lemon juice to prevent discoloration. Transfer the apples to a small roasting pan.

2. Place the blueberries and raisins in a bowl, then add the nuts, cinnamon, and sugar. Mix together well. Pile the mixture into the centers of the apple, then pour the wine over the apples.

3. Transfer the stuffed apples to the preheated oven and bake for 40–45 minutes, or until tender. Remove from the oven, then lift the apples out of the roasting pan and keep warm.

4. Blend the cornstarch with the water, then add the mixture to the cooking juices in the roasting pan. Transfer to the stove and cook over medium heat, stirring, until thickened. Remove from the heat and pour glaze over the apples. Serve the apples with heavy cream, if using.

1

2

2

SOMETHING
DIFFERENT
Bake the apples
in elderflower
wine or grape
juice instead of
the red wine.

Sweet Pies & Breads

Pumpkin Pie

 SERVES 8    PREP TIME: 25 minutes    COOKING TIME: 1 hour

nutritional information per serving	630 cal, 42g fat, 21g sat fat, 33g total sugars, 0.98g salt

This traditional pie makes a wonderful dessert for Thanksgiving, but it's so good that you can prepare it at other times during the year.

INGREDIENTS

all-purpose flour, for dusting

1 sheet store-bought rolled dough pie crust, thawed, if frozen

1 (15-ounce) can pumpkin puree

2 eggs, lightly beaten

¾ cup sugar

1 teaspoon ground cinnamon

½ teaspoon ground ginger

¼ teaspoon ground cloves

½ teaspoon salt

1 (12-fluid-ounce) can evaporated milk

brandy whipped cream

1½ cups heavy cream

½ cup confectioners' sugar

1 tablespoon brandy, or to taste

1 tablespoon light rum or dark rum, or to taste

freshly grated nutmeg, to decorate

1. Preheat the oven to 400°F. Lightly dust a rolling pin with flour and use to roll out the dough on a lightly floured surface into a 12-inch circle. Line a deep 9-inch pie plate with the pastry, trimming off the excess. Line the pastry shell with parchment paper and fill with pie weights or dried beans.

2. Bake in the preheated oven for 10 minutes. Remove from the oven and take out the paper and weights. Reduce the oven temperature to 350°F.

3. Meanwhile, put the pumpkin puree, eggs, sugar, cinnamon, ginger, cloves, and salt into a bowl and beat together, then beat in the evaporated milk. Pour the mixture into the pastry shell, return to the oven, and bake for 40–50 minutes, until the filling is set and a knife inserted in the center comes out clean. Transfer to a wire rack and set aside to cool completely.

4. While the pie is baking, make the brandy whipped cream. Put the cream in a bowl and beat until it has thickened and increased in volume. Just as it starts to stiffen, sift in the confectioners' sugar and continue beating until it holds stiff peaks. Add the brandy and rum and beat, being careful not to overbeat or the mixture will separate. Cover and chill until required. When ready to serve, grate some nutmeg over the whipped cream. Serve the pie with the cream.

Apple Pie

 SERVES 6

 PREP TIME:
40 minutes
plus chilling

 COOKING TIME:
50 minutes

nutritional information per serving	567 cal, 28g fat, 13.5g sat fat, 32g total sugars, 0.5g salt

A golden pie crust filled to the brim with apples, sugar, and a hint of cinnamon—this is the ultimate apple pie!

INGREDIENTS

pie dough
2¾ cups all-purpose flour, plus extra for dusting

pinch of salt

6 tablespoons salted butter or margarine, diced

⅓ cup plus 1 tablespoon lard or vegetable shortening, diced

6 tablespoons cold water

beaten egg or milk, for glazing

filling
3–4 large cooking apples (about 1¾–2¼ pounds), such as Granny Smith, Golden Delicious, or Pippin, peeled, cored, and sliced

⅔ cup superfine sugar, plus extra for sprinkling

½–1 teaspoon ground cinnamon, apple pie spice, or ground ginger

1. To make the pie dough, sift the flour and salt into a mixing bowl. Add the butter and lard and rub in with your fingertips until the mixture resembles fine bread crumbs. Add the water and gather the mixture together into a dough. Wrap the dough in plastic wrap and chill in the refrigerator for 30 minutes.

2. Preheat the oven to 425°F. Roll out almost two-thirds of the dough thinly on a lightly floured surface and use to line a deep 9-inch pie plate.

3. To make the filling, place the apple slices, sugar, and spice in a bowl and mix together thoroughly. Pack the apple mixture into the pie shell; the filling can come up above the rim. Add 1–2 tablespoons of water, if needed, particularly if the apples are not juicy.

4. Roll out the remaining dough on a lightly floured surface to form a lid. Dampen the edges of the pie rim with water and position the lid, pressing the edges firmly together. Trim and crimp the edges. Use the trimmings to cut out leaves or other shapes to decorate the top of the pie. Dampen and attach. Glaze the top of the pie with beaten egg, make 1–2 slits in the top and place the pie plate on a baking sheet.

5. Bake in the preheated oven for 20 minutes, then reduce the temperature to 350°F and bake for an additional 30 minutes, or until the pastry is a light golden brown. Serve hot or cold, sprinkled with sugar.

1

3

4

Rich Chocolate Pies

 SERVES 8    PREP TIME: 30 minutes plus chilling    COOKING TIME: 20–25 minutes

nutritional information per serving	711 cal, 54g fat, 33g sat fat, 30g total sugars, 0.5g salt

Crisp and sweet pastry shells with a wickedly smooth and creamy dark chocolate filling, these pies are perfect for a special dinner party dessert.

INGREDIENTS

pie dough
1¾ cups all-purpose flour, plus extra for dusting

1 stick salted butter, diced

2 tablespoons confectioners' sugar

1 egg yolk

2–3 tablespoons cold water

filling
8 ounces semisweet chocolate, broken into pieces, plus extra to decorate

1 stick salted butter

⅓ cup confectioners' sugar

1¼ cups heavy cream

1. To make the pie dough, sift the flour into a large bowl. Add the butter and rub it in with your fingertips until the mixture resembles bread crumbs. Add the confectioners' sugar, egg yolk, and enough water to form a soft dough. Wrap the dough in plastic wrap and chill in the refrigerator for 15 minutes. Roll the dough out on a lightly floured surface and use to line eight 4-inch shallow mini tart pans. Chill the tart shells for 30 minutes.

2. Preheat the oven to 400°F. Prick the bottoms of the tart shells with a fork and line with a little crumpled aluminum foil. Bake in the preheated oven for 10 minutes, then remove the foil and bake for 5–10 minutes, or until crisp. Transfer to a wire rack to cool. Reduce the oven temperature to 325°F.

3. To make the filling, place the chocolate, butter, and confectioners' sugar in a heatproof bowl set over a saucepan of simmering water and heat until melted. Remove from the heat and stir in 1 cup of the heavy cream. Remove the shells from the pans and place on a baking sheet. Fill each pastry shell with the chocolate. Bake for 5 minutes. Cool, then chill until required. To serve, whip the remaining cream and pipe or spoon into the center of each tart. Grate the remaining semisweet chocolate and use to decorate.

Banana Cream Pie

 SERVES 10　 PREP TIME: 30 minutes plus chilling　 COOKING TIME: 20–25 minutes

nutritional information per serving	562 cal, 33g fat, 16.5g sat fat, 25g total sugars, 0.5g salt

Sliced bananas in a crisp pie crust, topped with a smooth vanilla pudding and mounds of cream— this pie is a real winner!

INGREDIENTS

flour, for dusting
1 store-bought rolled dough pie crust, thawed, if frozen
4 extra-large egg yolks
½ cup superfine sugar
¼ cup cornstarch
pinch of salt
2 cups whole milk
1 teaspoon vanilla extract
3 bananas
½ tablespoon lemon juice
1½ cups heavy cream, whipped with 3 tablespoons confectioners' sugar, to decorate

1. Preheat the oven to 400°F. Lightly flour a rolling pin and use to roll out the rolled dough on a lightly floured surface into a 12-inch circle. Line a 9-inch pie plate with the dough, then trim the excess dough around the rim and prick the bottom all over with a fork. Line the pastry shell with parchment paper and fill with pie weights or dried beans.

2. Bake in the preheated oven for 15 minutes, or until the pastry is lightly golden. Remove the paper and weights and prick the bottom again. Return to the oven and bake for another 5–10 minutes, or until golden and dry. Let cool completely on a wire rack.

3. Meanwhile, put the egg yolks, sugar, cornstarch, and salt into a bowl and beat until blended and pale. Beat in the milk and vanilla extract.

4. Pour the mixture into a heavy saucepan over medium–high heat and bring to a boil, stirring, until smooth and thick. Reduce the heat to low and simmer, stirring, for 2 minutes. Strain the vanilla pudding into a bowl and set aside to cool.

5. Slice the bananas, place in a bowl with the lemon juice, and mix together. Arrange them in the cooled pastry shell, then top with the vanilla pudding and chill in the refrigerator for at least 2 hours. Spread the cream over the top of the pie and serve immediately.

Latticed Cherry Pie

 SERVES 8    PREP TIME: 40 minutes plus chilling    COOKING TIME: 45 minutes

nutritional information per serving	345 cal, 12.5g fat, 7.5g sat fat, 37g total sugars, 0.4g salt

This colorful pie is full of juicy cherries in a sweet almond- and cherry brandy-flavored syrup.

INGREDIENTS

pie dough
1 cup plus 2 tablespoons all-purpose flour, plus extra for dusting

¼ teaspoon baking powder

½ teaspoon allspice

½ teaspoon salt

¼ cup superfine sugar

4 tablespoons unsalted butter, chilled and diced, plus extra for greasing

1 egg, beaten, plus extra for glazing

filling
6 cups pitted fresh cherries (2 pounds), or 2 (15-ounce) cans cherries, drained

¾ cup superfine sugar

½ teaspoon almond extract

2 teaspoons cherry brandy

¼ teaspoon allspice

2 tablespoons cornstarch

2 tablespoons water

2 tablespoons unsalted butter, melted

ice cream, to serve

1. To make the dough, sift the flour with the baking powder into a large bowl. Stir in the allspice, salt, and sugar. Rub in the butter until the mixture resembles fine bread crumbs, make a well in the center, pour in the egg, and mix into a dough. Cut the dough in half, and use your hands to roll each half into a ball. Wrap in plastic wrap and chill in the refrigerator for 30 minutes.

2. Preheat the oven to 425°F. Grease a 9-inch pie plate. Roll out the doughs into two circles on a floured surface, each 12 inches in diameter. Use one to line the pie plate.

3. To make the filling, put half the cherries and all the sugar in a saucepan. Bring to a simmer and stir in the almond extract, brandy, and allspice. In a bowl, mix the cornstarch and water into a paste. Stir the paste into the saucepan, then boil until the mixture thickens. Stir in the remaining cherries, pour into the pastry shell, then dot with the melted butter. Cut the remaining dough circle into strips ½ inch wide. Lay the strips over the filling, crossing to form a lattice. Trim and seal the edges with water. Use your fingers to crimp around the rim, then glaze the top with the beaten egg.

4. Cover the pie with aluminum foil, then bake for 30 minutes in the preheated oven. Remove from the oven, discard the foil, then bake for an additional 15 minutes, or until golden. Serve with ice cream.

1

3

3

Lemon Meringue Pie

 SERVES 8

 PREP TIME:
40 minutes
plus chilling

 COOKING TIME:
55 minutes

nutritional information
per serving — 300 cal, 12g fat, 6.5g sat fat, 27g total sugars, 0.25g salt

The beauty of this classic dessert is the way the sweet pastry shell and sugary meringue perfectly complement the deliciously tangy lemon filling.

INGREDIENTS

pie dough
1 cup plus 2 tablespoons all-purpose flour, plus extra for dusting

6 tablespoons salted butter, diced, plus extra for greasing

¼ cup confectioners' sugar, sifted

finely grated rind of ½ lemon

½ egg yolk, beaten

1½ tablespoons milk

filling
3 tablespoons cornstarch

1¼ cups water

juice and grated rind of 2 lemons

1 cup superfine sugar

2 eggs, separated

1. To make the dough, sift the flour into a bowl. Rub in the butter with your fingertips until the mixture resembles fine bread crumbs. Mix in the remaining pastry ingredients. Invert onto a lightly floured surface and knead briefly. Wrap in plastic wrap and chill in the refrigerator for 30 minutes.

2. Preheat the oven to 350°F. Grease an 8-inch tart pan. Roll out the dough to a thickness of ¼ inch on a lightly floured surface, then use it to line the bottom and sides of the pan. Prick all over with a fork, line with parchment paper, and fill with pie weights or dried beans. Bake in the preheated oven for 15 minutes. Remove the pastry shell from the oven and take out the paper and weights. Reduce the oven temperature to 300°F.

3. To make the filling, mix the cornstarch with a little of the water to form a paste. Put the remaining water in a saucepan. Stir in the lemon juice, lemon rind, and cornstarch paste. Bring to a boil, stirring. Cook for 2 minutes. Let cool slightly. Stir in ⅓ cup of the superfine sugar and the egg yolks, then pour into the pastry shell.

4. Beat the egg whites in a clean, grease-free bowl until they hold stiff peaks. Gradually beat in the remaining superfine sugar and spread over the pie. Bake for an additional 40 minutes. Remove from the oven, cool, and serve.

Mixed Berry Pies

 MAKES 24    PREP TIME:
30 minutes    COOKING TIME:
15 minutes

nutritional information per pie	104 cal, 6g fat, 2g sat fat, 4g total sugars, 0.2g salt

Celebrate the summer with these gorgeous red fruit pies. The soft fruit contrasts deliciously with the crisp pastry.

INGREDIENTS

butter, for greasing

3 cups mixed berries, such as hulled strawberries, raspberries, and red currants (if available)

2 teaspoons cornstarch

3 tablespoons superfine sugar, plus extra for sprinkling

grated rind of ½ lemon

1 (15-ounce) store-bought rolled dough pie crust, thawed, if frozen

all-purpose flour, for dusting

1 egg yolk mixed with 1 tablespoon water, to glaze

whipped cream, to serve

1. Preheat the oven to 350°F. Lightly grease two muffin pans.

2. Coarsely chop the strawberries and break up large raspberries. Put all the fruit in a mixing bowl and stir in the cornstarch, sugar, and lemon rind.

3. Roll the dough out thinly on a lightly floured surface. Using a fluted cookie cutter, stamp out 24 circles, each 2½ inches in diameter. Press these gently into the prepared pans, rerolling the trimmings as needed. Reserve some of the trimmings for decoration.

4. Brush the top edges of the pie shells with a little of the egg glaze, then spoon in the filling.

5. Roll the reserved dough out thinly on a lightly floured surface. Cut strips ½ inch wide. Arrange two strips over each pie, pressing the edges together well to seal, then use a cookie cutter to cut small stars and arrange these over the strips. Brush egg glaze over the dough and sprinkle with a little sugar.

6. Bake in the preheated oven for 15 minutes, or until golden. Let cool in the pans for 10 minutes, then loosen with a round-blade knife and transfer to a wire rack to cool. Serve warm or cold with whipped cream.

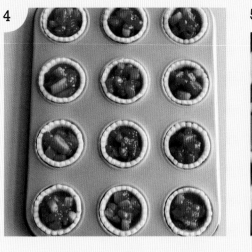

Peach Crumb Pie

 SERVES 6    PREP TIME: 45 minutes plus chilling    COOKING TIME: 40–45 minutes

nutritional information per serving	492 cal, 25g fat, 15g sat fat, 21g total sugars, 0.6g salt

This deep dish pie has juicy fresh peaches in a crisp pie crust with a buttery crumb topping.

INGREDIENTS

pie dough
1⅔ cups all-purpose flour, plus extra for dusting
1 stick salted butter, diced
1 egg yolk
1 teaspoon lemon juice
1–2 tablespoons iced water

crumb topping
1 cup all-purpose flour
1½ teaspoons baking powder
5 tablespoons salted butter, diced
¼ cup demerara sugar or other raw sugar

filling
4 just ripe peaches, halved, pitted, and sliced
2 tablespoons superfine sugar
1 tablespoon cornstarch

1. To make the pie dough, sift the flour into a bowl and add the butter. Rub the butter into the flour until the mixture resembles fine bread crumbs. Mix together the egg yolk and lemon juice with 1 tablespoon of the water. Stir into the flour mixture and mix to a firm dough, adding more water, if necessary. Knead lightly until smooth, then wrap in plastic wrap and chill in the refrigerator for 30 minutes.

2. Roll out the dough on a lightly floured work surface and use to line a 9-inch pie plate or loose-bottom round tart pan. Prick the bottom all over with a fork. Chill in the refrigerator for 15 minutes. Preheat the oven to 400°F and preheat a baking sheet.

3. Line the pastry shell with parchment paper and pie weights or dried beans. Place on the heated baking sheet and bake in the preheated oven for 10 minutes. Remove the paper and weights and bake for an additional 5–6 minutes, or until the pastry is light golden. Reduce the oven temperature to 375°F.

4. To make the crumb topping, place the flour, baking powder, and butter in a bowl and rub in the butter with your fingertips until crumbly. Stir in the sugar.

5. To make the filling, place the peach quarters in a bowl with the sugar and cornstarch and toss well to mix. Transfer to the pastry shell, then sprinkle the crumb topping over the filling.

6. Bake in the preheated oven for 25–30 minutes, or until the topping is golden. Serve warm or cold.

2

4

5

Mini Apple Pies

 MAKES 24    PREP TIME: 35 minutes    COOKING TIME: 15 minutes

nutritional information per pie	107 cal, 5.5g fat, 2g sat fat, 6g total sugars, 0.2g salt

If you prefer, cook these pies in advance and freeze when cool, then heat to warm up when needed.

INGREDIENTS

2 large cooking apples (1 pound), such as Granny Smith, Golden Delicious, or Pippin, cored, peeled, and diced

2 tablespoons salted butter, plus extra for greasing

¼ cup superfine sugar, plus extra for sprinkling

⅓ cup raisins or golden raisins

grated rind of 1 lemon

3 tablespoons Bourbon or brandy

1½ sheets store-bought rolled dough pie crust, thawed, if frozen

all-purpose flour, for dusting

milk, to glaze

whipped cream, to serve

1. Preheat the oven to 350°F. Lightly grease two muffin pans.

2. Put the apples in a skillet with the butter, sugar, raisins, and lemon rind. Cook, uncovered, over a gentle heat, stirring from time to time, for 8–10 minutes, or until the apples have softened but still hold their shape. Add the Bourbon and cook until just bubbling. Keeping it over the heat, flame with a taper or long match, stand well back, and cook for a minute or so, or until the flame subsides. Let the mixture cool.

3. Roll out half the dough thinly on a lightly floured surface. Using a fluted cookie cutter, stamp out 24 circles, each 2½ inches in diameter. Press these gently into the prepared pans, rerolling the trimmings as needed.

4. Brush the top edges of the pie shells with milk, then spoon in the filling, doming it up high in the center.

5. Roll out the reserved dough thinly on a lightly floured surface. Stamp out 24 circles, the same size as before, rerolling the trimmings as needed. Arrange these on top of the pies, pressing the edges together well to seal. Brush milk over the dough.

6. Shape tiny ropes from the remaining dough into the initials of your dinner guests or family. Press these onto the pie tops, brush with a little extra milk, and sprinkle with sugar.

7. Bake in the preheated oven for 15 minutes, or until golden. Let cool in the pans for 10 minutes, then loosen with a round-blade knife and transfer to a wire rack to cool. Serve warm or cold, sprinkled with a little extra sugar, with spoonfuls of whipped cream.

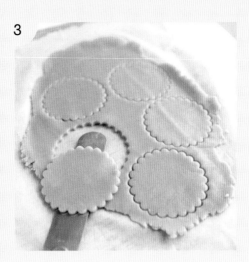

Key Lime Pie

 SERVES 8

 PREP TIME:
30 minutes
plus chilling

 COOKING TIME:
20 minutes

nutritional information
per serving

377 cal, 19g fat, 10g sat fat, 33g total sugars, 0.7g salt

This refreshing sweet lime pie originates from the Florida Keys and is named after the limes that are grown in the area.

INGREDIENTS

crumb crust
25 Graham crackers or gingersnaps (6 ounces)
2 tablespoons superfine sugar
½ teaspoon ground cinnamon
5 tablespoons salted butter, melted, plus extra for greasing

filling
1 (14-ounce) can condensed milk
½ cup freshly squeezed lime juice
finely grated rind of 3 limes
4 egg yolks
whipped cream, to serve

1. Preheat the oven to 325°F. Lightly grease a 9-inch tart pan, about 1½ inches deep. To make the crumb crust, put the cookies, sugar, and cinnamon in a food processor and process until fine crumbs form—do not overprocess to a powder. Add the melted butter and process again until moistened.

2. Transfer the crumb mixture to the prepared tart pan and press over the bottom and up the sides. Place the tart pan on a baking sheet and bake in the preheated oven for 5 minutes. Meanwhile, to make the filling, beat together the condensed milk, lime juice, lime rind, and egg yolks in a bowl until well blended.

3. Remove the tart pan from the oven, pour the filling into the crumb crust, and spread out to the edges. Return to the oven for an additional 15 minutes, or until the filling is set around the edges but still wobbly in the center. Let cool completely on a wire rack, then cover and chill for at least 2 hours. Spread with whipped cream and serve.

SOMETHING
DIFFERENT

Instead of cream, top the pie with meringue and brown briefly in a hot oven.

Maple & Pecan Pie

 SERVES 8

 PREP TIME:
40 minutes
plus chilling

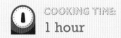 COOKING TIME:
1 hour

nutritional information
per serving | 578 cal, 39g fat, 13g sat fat, 32g total sugars, 0.6g salt

This classic favorite tastes great served warm with a scoop of vanilla ice cream.

INGREDIENTS

pie dough
1⅓ cups plus 1 tablespoon
all-purpose flour, plus extra
for dusting
6 tablespoons salted butter, diced
1 tablespoon superfine sugar
1 egg, beaten with 1 tablespoon
cold water

filling
6 tablespoons salted butter
⅓ cup firmly packed
light brown sugar
⅔ cup maple syrup
⅓ cup corn syrup
3 extra-large eggs, beaten
1 teaspoon vanilla extract
2 cups pecan halves

1. To make the dough, sift the flour into a bowl and add the butter. Rub the butter into the flour until the mixture resembles fine bread crumbs. Stir in the superfine sugar and egg-and-water mixture and mix to a firm dough.

2. Place the dough on a lightly floured work surface and lightly knead until smooth. Roll out and use to line a 9-inch loose-bottom tart pan. Prick the dough all over with a fork and chill in the refrigerator for 30 minutes. Meanwhile, preheat the oven to 400°F.

3. Place the pan on a baking sheet and line with parchment paper and pie weights or dried beans. Bake in the preheated oven for 10 minutes, then remove the paper and weights and bake for an additional 5 minutes, or until the pastry is light golden. Reduce the oven temperature to 350°F.

4. To make the filling, place the butter, brown sugar, maple syrup, and corn syrup in a saucepan and heat over low heat until melted. Let cool for 5 minutes, then beat in the eggs and vanilla extract. Chop half of the pecans and stir into the mixture.

5. Pour the filling into the pastry shell and sprinkle with the remaining nuts. Bake in the preheated oven for 35–45 minutes, or until the filling is just set. Serve warm or cold.

3

4

5

Banana & Caramel Pie

 SERVES 10    PREP TIME: 2½ hours plus cooling    COOKING TIME: 10–12 minutes

nutritional information per serving	880 cal, 54g fat, 31g sat fat, 78g total sugars, 0.8g salt

This scrumptious dessert is a real crowd pleaser with a nutty cookie crust, sliced bananas, gooey caramel sauce, and a mountain of whipped cream.

INGREDIENTS

filling
3 (14-ounce) cans sweetened condensed milk

4 ripe bananas

juice of ½ lemon

1 teaspoon vanilla extract

3 ounces semisweet chocolate, grated

2 cups heavy cream, whipped

cookie crust
6 tablespoons salted butter, melted, plus extra for greasing

1¼ cups finely crushed Graham crackers

¼ cup almonds, toasted and ground

¼ cup hazelnuts, toasted and ground

1. Place the unopened cans of milk in a large saucepan and add enough water to cover them. Bring to a boil, then reduce the heat and simmer for 2 hours, filling up the water level to keep the cans covered. Carefully lift out the hot cans from the pan and let cool.

2. Preheat the oven to 350°F and grease a 9-inch tart pan. To make the crust, place the butter in a bowl and add the crushed cookies and ground nuts. Mix together well, then press the mixture evenly into the bottom and sides of the prepared tart pan. Bake in the preheated oven for 10–12 minutes. Let cool.

3. Peel and slice the bananas and place in a bowl. Squeeze the juice from the lemon over the sliced bananas, add the vanilla extract, and mix together. Spread the banana mixture over the cookie crust in the pan, then spoon the contents of the cooled cans of condensed milk over the filling.

4. Sprinkle with two-thirds of the chocolate, then top with a layer of whipped cream. Sprinkle the remaining grated chocolate over the cream and serve the pie at room temperature.

Chocolate Peanut Butter Pie

 SERVES 8

 PREP TIME:
40 minutes
plus chilling

 COOKING TIME:
10 minutes

nutritional information per serving	724 cal, 61g fat, 35g sat fat, 28g total sugars, 0.7g salt

If you love peanut butter and chocolate, then this decadent cream pie is just right for you!

INGREDIENTS

cookie crust
2 cups finely crushed chocolate cookies

2 ounces semisweet chocolate, grated

5 tablespoons salted butter, melted

filling
¾ cup cream cheese

½ cup smooth peanut butter

2 tablespoons superfine sugar

1 cup heavy cream

chocolate glaze
4 ounces semisweet chocolate, broken into pieces

1 tablespoon corn syrup

2 tablespoons unsalted butter

½ cup heavy cream

chopped roasted peanuts, to decorate

1. Preheat the oven to 350°F.

2. Put the cookie crumbs into a bowl and stir in the grated chocolate and melted butter. Press the mixture into the bottom and up the sides of a 9-inch tart pan. Bake in the preheated oven for 10 minutes, or until just set. Let cool.

3. To make the filling, put the cream cheese and peanut butter into a bowl and beat together until smooth. Beat in the sugar, then gradually beat in the cream. Spoon the mixture into the cookie crust and gently level the surface. Chill in the refrigerator for 30 minutes.

4. To make the glaze, put the chocolate, syrup, and butter into a heatproof bowl set over a saucepan of simmering water and heat until melted. Remove from the heat and stir in the cream until smooth. Let cool for 10–20 minutes, or until thickened, then gently spread over the filling. Chill in the refrigerator for at least 1 hour before serving.

5. To serve, remove the pie from the pan and decorate with chopped roasted peanuts.

Coconut Cream Pie

 SERVES 6

 PREP TIME:
30 minutes
plus chilling

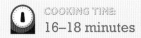 COOKING TIME:
16–18 minutes

nutritional information per serving	753 cal, 62g fat, 37g sat fat, 12g total sugars, 0.6g salt

A simple pie crust filled with a layer of sweet coconut and vanilla pudding and topped with whipped cream and lightly toasted coconut.

INGREDIENTS

1 sheet store-bought rolled dough pie crust, thawed, if frozen

2 eggs

¼ cup superfine sugar

1 teaspoon vanilla extract

2 tablespoons all-purpose flour, plus extra for dusting

2 tablespoons cornstarch

⅔ cup whole milk

1 cup coconut milk

⅓ cup dry unsweetened coconut

1¾ cups heavy cream

2 tablespoons toasted dry unsweetened coconut, to decorate

1. Preheat the oven to 400°F. Roll the dough out on a lightly floured surface and use to line an 8–9-inch pie plate. Trim and crimp the edges. Prick the bottom with a fork and chill in the refrigerator for 15 minutes.

2. Line the pastry shell with parchment paper and pie weights or dried beans. Bake in the preheated oven for 10 minutes. Remove the paper and weights and bake for an additional 6–8 minutes, or until golden. Let cool.

3. For the filling, beat together the eggs, sugar, and vanilla extract in a bowl. Blend the flour and cornstarch to a paste with ¼ cup of milk, then beat the paste into the egg mixture. Heat the remaining milk and coconut milk in a saucepan until almost boiling and pour onto the egg mixture, stirring continuously. Return to the saucepan and slowly heat, beating until smooth and thick. Stir in the coconut. Cover with dampened wax paper and let stand until cold.

4. Spread the coconut filling in the pastry shell. Whip the cream until holding soft peaks and spread over the top of the filling. Sprinkle with the toasted coconut and serve.

Crusty White Loaf

 MAKES
1 loaf

 PREP TIME:
20 minutes
plus rising

 COOKING TIME:
30 minutes

nutritional information per loaf	2,123 cal, 42g fat, 18g sat fat, 17g total sugars, 7.7g salt

Baking your own bread is a satisfying and rewarding pastime. If you're a novice baker, then start with this simple white loaf.

INGREDIENTS

1 egg
1 egg yolk
⅔–1 cup lukewarm water
3⅔ cups white bread flour, plus extra for dusting
1½ teaspoons salt
2 teaspoons sugar
1 teaspoon active dry yeast
2 tablespoons salted butter, diced
sunflower oil, for greasing

1. Place the egg and egg yolk in a bowl and beat lightly to mix. Add enough lukewarm water to make up to 1¼ cups. Stir well.

2. Place the flour, salt, sugar, and yeast in a large bowl. Add the butter and rub it in with your fingertips until the mixture resembles bread crumbs. Make a well in the center, add the egg mixture, and work to a smooth dough.

3. Invert onto a lightly floured surface and knead well for about 10 minutes, or until smooth. Brush a bowl with oil. Shape the dough into a ball, place it in the bowl, and cover with a damp dish towel. Let rise in a warm place for 1 hour, or until the dough has doubled in volume. Preheat the oven to 425°F. Oil a 9-inch loaf pan. Invert the dough onto a lightly floured surface and knead for 1 minute, or until smooth. Shape the dough the length of the pan and three times the width. Fold the dough into three lengthwise and place it in the pan with the seam underneath. Cover and let rest in a warm place for 30 minutes, or until it has risen above the pan.

4. Place in the preheated oven and bake for 30 minutes, or until firm and golden brown. Test that the loaf is cooked by tapping on the base with your knuckles—it should sound hollow. Transfer to a wire rack to cool.

2

3

3

Whole-Wheat Loaf

 MAKES
1 loaf

 PREP TIME:
20 minutes
plus rising

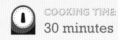 COOKING TIME:
30 minutes

nutritional information per loaf	1,024 cal, 27g fat, 3g sat fat, 34g total sugars, 5g salt

Made with whole-wheat flour, which contains the whole wheat grain, this loaf will have more flavor, fiber, and nutrients than white bread.

INGREDIENTS

1⅔ cups whole-wheat bread flour, plus extra for dusting

1 tablespoon powdered milk

1 teaspoon salt

2 tablespoons light brown sugar

1 teaspoon active dry yeast

1½ tablespoons sunflower oil, plus extra for greasing

¾ cup lukewarm water

1. Place the flour, powdered milk, salt, sugar, and yeast in a large bowl. Pour in the oil and add the water, then mix well to make a smooth dough.

2. Invert onto a lightly floured surface and knead well for about 10 minutes, or until smooth. Brush a bowl with oil. Shape the dough into a ball, place it in the bowl, and cover with a damp dish towel. Let rise in a warm place for 1 hour, or until the dough has doubled in volume.

3. Preheat the oven to 425°F. Oil a 9-inch loaf pan. Invert the dough onto a lightly floured surface and knead for 1 minute, or until smooth. Shape the dough the length of the pan and three times the width. Fold the dough into three lengthwise and place it in the pan with the seam underneath. Cover and let stand in a warm place for 30 minutes, or until it has risen above the pan.

4. Place in the preheated oven and bake for 30 minutes, or until firm and golden brown. Test that the loaf is cooked by tapping on the base with your knuckles—it should sound hollow. Transfer to a wire rack to cool.

1

2

3

Sourdough Bread

 MAKES
2 loaves

 PREP TIME:
30 minutes plus
starter and rising

 COOKING TIME:
30 minutes

nutritional information per loaf	1,302 cal, 23g fat, 5g sat fat, 49g total sugars, 10.3g salt

You'll need to plan ahead to make this rustic bread by preparing the starter dough a few days in advance.

INGREDIENTS

3¾ cups whole-wheat flour

4 teaspoons salt

1½ cups lukewarm water

2 tablespoons dark molasses

1 tablespoon vegetable oil, plus extra for brushing

all-purpose flour, for dusting

starter

¾ cup whole-wheat flour

⅔ cup white bread flour

¼ cup superfine sugar

1 cup plus 1 tablespoon whole milk

1. For the starter, put the whole-wheat flour, white bread flour, sugar, and milk into a nonmetallic bowl and beat well with a fork. Cover with a damp dish towel and let stand at room temperature for 4–5 days, until the mixture is frothy and smells sour.

2. Sift together the flour and half the salt into a bowl and add the water, molasses, oil, and starter. Mix well with a wooden spoon until a dough begins to form, then knead with your hands until it leaves the side of the bowl. Invert onto a lightly floured surface and knead for 10 minutes, or until smooth and elastic.

3. Brush a bowl with oil. Form the dough into a ball, put it into the bowl, and put the bowl into a plastic food bag or cover with a damp dish towel. Let rise in a warm place for 2 hours, or until the dough has doubled in volume.

4. Dust two baking sheets with flour. Mix the remaining salt with ¼ cup of water in a bowl. Invert the dough onto a lightly floured surface and punch down with your fist to knock out the air, then knead for 10 minutes. Halve the dough, shape each piece into an oval, and place the loaves on the prepared baking sheets. Brush with the salty water glaze and let stand in a warm place, brushing frequently with the glaze, for 30 minutes.

5. Preheat the oven to 425°F. Brush the loaves with the remaining glaze and bake for 30 minutes, or until the crust is golden brown and the loaves sound hollow when tapped on their bottoms with your knuckles. If it is necessary to cook them for longer, reduce the oven temperature to 375°F. Transfer to wire racks to cool.

Five-Grain Loaf

 MAKES
1 loaf

 PREP TIME:
20 minutes
plus rising

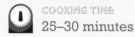 COOKING TIME:
25–30 minutes

nutritional information per loaf	2,544 cal, 84g fat, 12g sat fat, 24g total sugars, 4.8g salt

Packed full of nutritious seeds and made with whole-wheat flour, this loaf is full of fiber.

INGREDIENTS

2¼ cups whole-wheat bread flour, plus extra for dusting

1⅔ cups white bread flour

1 teaspoon salt

⅔ cup mixed seeds, including sesame, pumpkin, sunflower, hemp, and flax seeds

2¼ teaspoons active dry yeast

1 tablespoon light brown sugar

2 tablespoons sunflower oil, plus extra for greasing

1¼ cups lukewarm water

1. Lightly grease a baking sheet with oil. Mix the whole-wheat flour, white flour, salt, mixed seeds, and yeast in a large bowl. Stir in the sugar. Mix together the oil and water. Make a well in the center of the dry ingredients and pour in the liquid ingredients. Mix with a knife to make a soft, sticky dough.

2. Invert the dough onto a lightly floured surface and knead for 5–7 minutes, or until smooth and elastic. Shape the dough into a round ball and place on the prepared baking sheet. Dust the top of the loaf with whole-wheat flour and let stand in a warm place for 1–1½ hours, or until doubled in size.

3. Meanwhile, preheat the oven to 425°F. Bake in the preheated oven for 5 minutes. Reduce the oven temperature to 400°F and bake for an additional 20–25 minutes, or until golden brown and the bottom sounds hollow when tapped with your knuckles. Transfer to a wire rack to cool.

1

2

3

SOMETHING
DIFFERENT
To make individual
rolls, divide and
shape the dough
into 12 round balls
and bake for
10-15 minutes
at 400°F.

Oatmeal Bread

 MAKES
1 loaf

 PREP TIME:
20 minutes
plus rising

 COOKING TIME:
25–30 minutes

nutritional information per loaf	1,872 cal, 36g fat, 18g sat fat, 24g total sugars, 7.2g salt

This is an easy-to-make country loaf with a wonderful soft texture and nutty flavor.

INGREDIENTS

¾ cup rolled oats, plus extra for sprinkling

1⅔ cups white bread flour, plus extra for dusting

1¼ cups whole-wheat bread flour

1½ teaspoons salt

2¼ teaspoons active dry yeast

2 tablespoons salted butter, diced

1 tablespoon light brown sugar

1¼ cups lukewarm water

sunflower oil, for greasing

1. Mix together the oats, white flour, whole-wheat flour, salt, and yeast in a large bowl. Add the butter and rub in to make fine bread crumbs. Stir in the sugar. Make a well in the center and pour in the water. Mix with a knife to make a soft, sticky dough. Invert the dough onto a lightly floured surface and knead for 5–7 minutes, or until smooth and elastic. Place in a bowl, cover with oiled plastic wrap, and let stand in a warm place for about 1 hour, or until doubled in size. Lightly grease a baking sheet with oil.

2. Invert the risen dough onto a floured surface and lightly knead again for 1 minute. Shape into a 10-inch oblong and place on the prepared baking sheet. Slash the top of the loaf six to eight times with a sharp knife. Cover loosely with oiled plastic wrap and let stand in a warm place for 30 minutes, or until doubled in size again.

3. Meanwhile, preheat the oven to 425°F. Lightly brush the loaf with water and sprinkle with a handful of oats. Bake in the preheated oven for 25–30 minutes, or until golden brown and the bottom sounds hollow when tapped. Transfer to a wire rack to cool.

1

1

2

FREEZING TIP
Wrap in foil
and freeze for
up to one month.
Thaw at room
temperature for
3-4 hours.

Cornbread

 MAKES
1 loaf

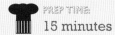 PREP TIME:
15 minutes

 COOKING TIME:
30–35 minutes

nutritional information per loaf	3.247 cal, 171g fat, 89g sat fat, 19g total sugars, 12.8g salt

Cornmeal gives this yeast-free bread a wonderful golden color and distinctive flavor.

INGREDIENTS

vegetable oil, for greasing
1⅓ cups all-purpose flour
1 teaspoon salt
4 teaspoons baking powder
1 teaspoon superfine sugar
2 cups cornmeal
1 stick salted butter, softened
4 eggs
1 cup whole milk
3 tablespoons heavy cream

1. Preheat the oven to 400°F. Brush an 8-inch square cake pan with oil.

2. Sift together the flour, salt, and baking powder into a bowl. Add the sugar and cornmeal and stir to mix. Add the butter and cut into the dry ingredients with a knife, then rub it in with your fingertips until the mixture resembles fine bread crumbs.

3. Lightly beat the eggs in a bowl with the milk and cream, then stir into the cornmeal mixture until thoroughly combined.

4. Spoon the dough into the prepared pan and smooth the surface. Bake in the preheated oven for 30–35 minutes, or until a toothpick inserted into the center of the loaf comes out clean. Remove the pan from the oven and let cool for 5–10 minutes, then cut into squares and serve warm.

Spiced Fruit Loaf

 MAKES
1 loaf

 PREP TIME:
20 minutes
plus rising

COOKING TIME:
1 hour 10 mins

nutritional information per loaf	3.810 cal, 120g fat, 66g sat fat, 306g total sugars, 2.4g salt

This sweet and spiced fruit bread is delicious served lightly toasted and spread with butter and preserves.

INGREDIENTS

3⅓ cups white bread flour, plus extra for dusting

pinch of salt

2 teaspoons allspice

1 stick unsalted butter, diced

2¼ teaspoons easy-blend dried yeast

½ cup unrefined superfine sugar

¾ cup dried currants

¾ cup raisins

¼ cup chopped candied peel

finely grated rind of 1 orange

1 egg, beaten

⅔ cup whole milk, warmed

vegetable oil, for oiling

1. Sift the flour, salt, and allspice into a bowl and rub in the butter until the mixture resembles bread crumbs. Stir in the yeast, sugar, dried fruit, candied peel, and orange rind, then add the egg and the warm milk and bring together to form a soft dough.

2. Knead the dough briefly on a lightly floured surface. Flour a clean bowl and add the dough. Cover the bowl and let rise in a warm place for 2 hours.

3. Preheat the oven to 350°F and oil a 9-inch loaf pan. Knead the dough again briefly, then place it in the prepared pan, cover, and let rise for 20 minutes. Bake in the preheated oven for 1 hour 10 minutes—the loaf should be golden and well risen. Let cool in the pan before slicing and serving.

1

2
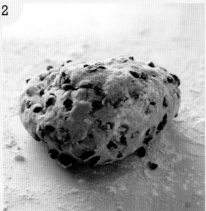

3

SOMETHING DIFFERENT
Add chopped preserved ginger to the dough and glaze the warm loaf with the syrup.

Seeded Rye Bread

 MAKES
1 loaf

 PREP TIME:
25 minutes
plus rising

 COOKING TIME:
30–35 minutes

nutritional information per loaf	2,040 cal, 36g fat, 12g sat fat, 36g total sugars, 7.2g salt

This dense loaf made with rye flour and dotted with caraway seeds is best served thinly sliced on the day of making.

INGREDIENTS

2½ cups rye flour, plus extra for dusting

2 cups white bread flour

1½ teaspoons salt

1 tablespoon caraway seeds

2¼ teaspoons active dry yeast

2 tablespoons salted butter, melted

2 tablespoons honey, warmed

1¼ cups lukewarm water

sunflower oil, for greasing

1. Mix the rye flour, white flour, salt, caraway seeds, and yeast in a large bowl and make a well in the center. Mix together the butter, honey, and water and pour into the well. Mix with a knife to make a soft, sticky dough. Lightly grease a baking sheet with oil.

2. Invert the dough onto a floured surface and knead for 10 minutes, or until smooth and elastic. Shape into an oval and place on the prepared baking sheet. Slash the top of the loaf in a diamond pattern, lightly dust with flour and let stand in a warm place for 1–1½ hours, or until doubled in size.

3. Meanwhile, preheat the oven to 375°F. Bake in the preheated oven for 30–35 minutes, or until the crust is a rich brown and the bottom of the loaf sounds hollow when tapped with your knuckles. Transfer to a wire rack to cool.

1

2

2

GOES WELL WITH

Spread a little mayonnaise on thin slices of the bread, then top with ruffles of smoked salmon, sliced avocado, and a squeeze of lemon juice.

Bread Rolls

 MAKES 12  PREP TIME: 30 minutes plus rising 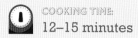 COOKING TIME: 12–15 minutes

nutritional information per roll	173 cal, 7g fat, 4g sat fat, 2g total sugars, 0.3g salt

These crusty golden bread rolls are particularly good served warm with a steaming bowl of soup.

INGREDIENTS

½ cup whole milk

¼ cup water

5 tablespoons butter, softened, plus extra for brushing

2½ cups white bread flour, plus extra for dusting

2¼ teaspoons active dry yeast

1 tablespoon sugar

½ teaspoon salt

1 extra-large egg, beaten

sunflower oil, for greasing

1. Put the milk, water, and 2 tablespoons of the butter into a small saucepan and heat to 110–120°F. Put the flour, yeast, sugar, and salt into a large bowl, stir, and make a well in the center. Slowly pour in ⅓ cup of the milk mixture, then add the egg and beat, drawing in the flour from the side. Add the remaining milk, tablespoon by tablespoon, until a soft dough forms.

2. Grease a bowl and set aside. Invert the dough onto a lightly floured surface and knead for 8–10 minutes, or until smooth and elastic. Shape the dough into a ball, roll it around in the greased bowl, cover with plastic wrap, and set aside for 1 hour, or until doubled in size.

3. Invert the dough onto a lightly floured surface and punch down to knock out the air. Cover with the upturned bowl and let rest for 10 minutes. Meanwhile, preheat the oven to 400°F and dust a baking sheet with flour. Melt the remaining butter in a small saucepan over medium heat.

4. Lightly dust a rolling pin with flour and use to roll out the dough to a thickness of ¼ inch. Use a floured 3¼-inch round cookie cutter to cut out 12 circles, rerolling the trimmings, if necessary. Brush the middle of a circle with butter. Use a floured chopstick or pencil to make an indentation just off center, then fold along that indentation and pinch the edges together to seal. Place on the prepared baking sheet, cover with a dish towel, and let rise while you shape the remaining rolls.

5. Lightly brush the tops of the rolls with butter and bake in the preheated oven for 12–15 minutes, or until the rolls are golden brown and the bottoms sound hollow when tapped. Transfer to a wire rack to cool.

Seeded Bread Rolls

 MAKES 8    PREP TIME: 15 minutes plus rising   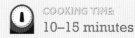 COOKING TIME: 10–15 minutes

nutritional information per roll	221 cal, 4g fat, 0.5g sat fat, 1g total sugars, 0.7g salt

Delicious split and buttered while still warm, these seeded rolls taste so much better than store-bought rolls.

INGREDIENTS

3⅓ cups white bread flour, plus extra for dusting

1 teaspoon salt

2¼ teaspoons active dry yeast

1 tablespoon vegetable oil, plus extra for brushing

1½ cups lukewarm water

1 egg, beaten

sesame seeds or poppy seeds, for sprinkling

1. Place the flour, salt, and yeast in a large bowl and mix well. Pour in the oil and add the water, then mix well to make a smooth dough.

2. Invert onto a lightly floured surface and knead well for 5–7 minutes, or until smooth and elastic. Brush a bowl with oil. Shape the dough into a ball, place it in the bowl, and cover with a damp dish towel. Let rise in a warm place for 1 hour, or until the dough has doubled in volume.

3. Invert the dough onto a lightly floured surface and knead briefly until smooth. Divide the dough into eight pieces. Shape half the dough into round rolls. Make the other half into rolls with a small round shape on top for variation, if you desire. Place the rolls on a baking sheet.

4. Cover the rolls with a damp dish towel and let rise for 30 minutes, or until the rolls have doubled in size.

5. Preheat the oven to 425°F. Brush the rolls with the beaten egg and sprinkle with seeds. Bake in the preheated oven for 10–15 minutes, or until golden brown. Test that the rolls are cooked by tapping on the bottoms with your knuckles—they should sound hollow. Transfer to a wire rack to cool.

2

3

5

Index